CROCHET WITH
BEADS

Ruth Herring

CROCHET WITH
BEADS

18 STUNNING PROJECTS FOR JEWELLERY AND ACCESSORIES

NEW
HOLLAND

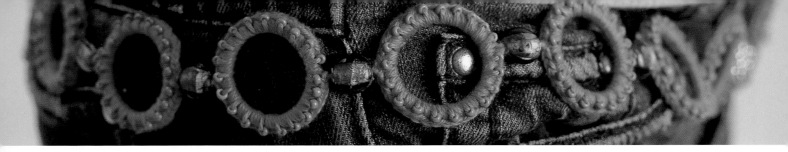

First published in 2007 by New Holland Publishers (UK) Ltd
London • Cape Town • Sydney • Auckland
Garfield House
86–88 Edgware Road
London W2 2EA
United Kingdom
www.newhollandpublishers.com

80 McKenzie Street
Cape Town 8001
South Africa

Unit 1, 66 Gibbes Street
Chatswood, NSW 2067
Australia

218 Lake Road
Northcote, Auckland
New Zealand

ISBN   978 1 84537 672 7

Senior Editor **Corinne Masciocchi**
Designer **Lisa Tai**
Photographer **Shona Wood**
Production **Marion Storz**
Editorial Direction **Rosemary Wilkinson**

10 9 8 7 6 5 4 3 2 1

Reproduction by Pica Digital, Pte Ltd, Singapore
Printed and bound by Craft Print International Ltd, Singapore

CONTENTS

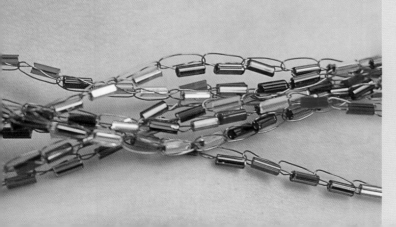

Introduction

When I was commissioned to undertake this project, I didn't know where to start. The sheer choice of beads and the number of outlets was overwhelming. It was very tempting to concentrate on the stunning statement beads on offer, but I quickly found that not only would it make some of the projects' cost prohibitive, but also the weight of some of the larger beads had a tendency to drag rather than hang from the crochet stitches.

Instead I have opted to design projects using a few statement beads with a wide assortment of cheaper beads, including seed beads, bugle beads, discs and sequins. Not only are these beads available in a multitude of colours and sizes, they can be bought in a wide variety of outlets, from major department stores to small sewing shops and markets.

Gone are the days when crochet was used almost exclusively for producing doilies for the side table and granny squares for dog basket blankets. These days the doilies are crocheted together to form stunning dresses for the catwalk and granny squares are worked in the finest yarns to produce wonderful throws for the sofa. These beaded crochet projects prove that an evening's work can produce a piece of jewellery to add instant glamour to anyone's wardrobe.

For me, the beauty of working with crochet is its portability. Small projects like the ones in this book can be kept in a handbag or a small rucksack and can be worked on at any opportunity – now it is considered trendy to crochet in the coolest hostelries in the most urban of surroundings. Furthermore, fellow passengers won't be subjected to bruised arms or annoying clicking if you choose to make good use of your commuting time. Indeed, many of the projects in this book were conceived and executed on the move! I hope you enjoy making the projects in this book and that they will inspire you to make your own dazzling creations.

MATERIALS, EQUIPMENT AND TECHNIQUES

1 materials and equipment

The following pages will help you make informed decisions when it comes to buying beads, yarn and equipment for your projects. It is possible to start with purchasing just one hook and a couple of different size sewing needles.

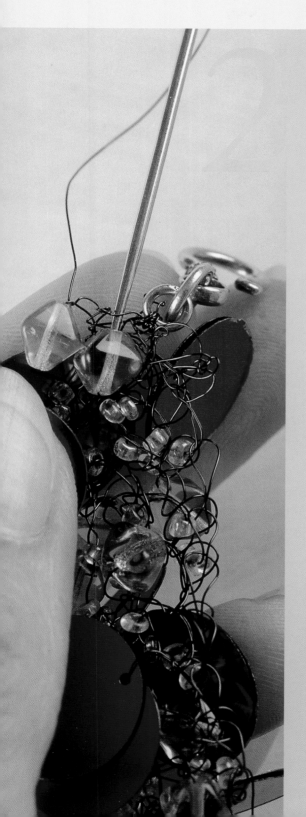

techniques

Many of the projects in this book can be attempted by mastering a few very basic crochet stitches and techniques. Follow the step-by-step instructions to practise the stitches before progressing onto the jewellery pieces, which start with the simplest project first.

Materials

The choice of the materials used in a project plays a huge part in the overall design process. A few simple crochet stitches can be transformed into something very special with some stunning beads and a spool of cotton or wire. Experiment with contrasting or co-ordinating materials to create quite different effects to suit different tastes. The beauty of making jewellery pieces is they are quick to produce and use small quantities of materials, allowing statement beads to be included to add a wow factor.

Beads

Hunting for beads can be a daunting task, with catalogues listing beads under different categories and to make things more confusing, retailers using different names for the finishes! Here is a list of the types of glass beads available, giving the alternative names and a brief description of the finishes.

SEED BEADS OR ROCAILLES

You may find some seed beads sold as rocailles. They are essentially the same thing – small glass beads that can be used for fine crochet and knitting, embroidery, weaving and jewellery making. The only noticeable difference is that rocailles have a square as opposed to a round hole, which is often silver-lined (*see* Bead finishes, page 12).

Seed beads are manufactured in India, Japan, Taiwan and the Czech Republic, and have slightly different characteristics depending on the country of origin. Generally, the Czech beads are more rounded than the more cylindrical shapes from the Asia Pacific countries, with the Japanese beads being more regular in shape than those from Taiwan. Indian beads are normally the most irregular.

Seed beads are sized by number – the smaller the number, the larger the bead. The smallest seed beads used in these projects are a size 10/0, where they have been used with wire, and the largest, a size 5/0, used with crochet cotton.

BUGLE BEADS

Bugle beads are lengths of cut glass cane available in sizes ranging from 2 mm to 30 mm. Bugle beads can be used with wire and with cottons up to a 4 ply thickness. If used with cotton, the beads will have to be threaded onto the yarns using the Threading beads onto crochet cotton technique on page 24.

PONY BEADS

These are like large seed beads in shape and are made in glass, plastic or wood. They are normally available in two sizes: 7 x 4 mm and 9 x 6 mm and are ideal for use with thicker cotton yarns, thonging and more unusual materials like raffia or plastic laces. Plastic pony beads can be bought very cheaply in single colours or in large mixed bags. They are brilliant to use for trying out ideas, before moving on to more costly glass versions and they make good stocking fillers for children interested in beadwork. Some unusual finishes like 'glow in the dark', 'sparkle' and 'neon' are available in plastic.

PRESSED GLASS BEADS

These are moulded beads that form unusual shapes and make a real statement to any piece. Normally larger in size, they can be found in a multitude of shapes: flattened ovals, twisted lozenges, rectangular, the list is endless and the exciting thing is that each bead outlet will have their own supplier manufacturing exclusive beads. Again, the finishes are breathtaking with some of the best being silver-lined and bi-coloured. They tend to have smaller holes than pony beads, limiting them to use with finer cottons and wire.

WIRED PENDANT BEADS

Adding wires to different shaped glass beads produces pretty pendant shapes which, like a drop bead, add movement to the jewellery. Wired beads can be purchased or you can add the wire yourself to your favourite beads.

FACETED BEADS

These are glass or plastic hand- or machine-cut beads. They are distinctive with their multiple flat faces that catch the light and give the beads an extra sparkle. Faceted drop beads have a hole pierced through the top, which allows them to dangle

ROCAILLES

SEED BEADS

BALL BUTTONS

PRESSED GLASS BEADS

BUGLE BEADS

WIRED HEART PENDANTS

SEQUINS

BLACK JET FACETED DROP BEADS

DISCS

PONY BEADS

WIRED PENDANTS

SQUARE SEQUINS

freely to give movement to the jewellery. They are available in many shapes, with bicones, hearts and teardrops being the most popular. Most bead outlets stock a range of cut-glass beads that imitate semi-precious stones like jet, amethyst, topaz, opal and tanzanite. If fine crystal does not suit your wallet, there are some wonderful plastic alternatives that come in a wide range of colours in both transparent and frosted finishes. The plastic alternatives are lighter, giving you the option of using large quantities of the bigger sizes available for impact without producing a finished piece that is too heavy.

BALL BUTTONS

These are not strictly beads, but round buttons that have a hole pierced through one end rather than having a shank. They are available from button shops and haberdashery departments in a wide range of colours.

SEQUINS AND DISCS

Sequins and discs are made from pressed pieces of thin plastic and are available in a variety of colours, sizes and shapes – round, square, oval, star, leaf, snowflake, faceted – the selection is limitless! The main difference between the two is that sequins have a central hole whereas discs have a hole at the top, which makes them better for hanging. Both have been used in this book in conjunction with bugle beads and seed beads to add extra sparkle.

DEGREES OF BEAD TRANSPARENCY

Glass beads come in various degrees of transparency:
Transparent or clear: beads transmit light and are therefore easy to see through even when they are coloured. They are available in many colours and are sometimes lined (*see* Bead finishes).
Translucent: you cannot see clearly through a translucent glass bead.
Opal: replicating the look of an opal gemstone, these beads transmit light with the milky, translucent effect produced by the addition of fluorides to the molten glass.
Opaque: this is the name given for glass beads that you cannot see through.

BEAD FINISHES

Once the transparency has been selected, the bead can have a range of finishes added, as described below.
Colour-lined: these beads are made with transparent glass with the inside of the hole dyed or painted with an opaque colour. The resulting effect is a greatly enhanced bead colour.
Silver-lined: silver-lined beads have a mirror-like reflective lining in their holes to enhance the colour of the bead. Beads with silver-lined square holes (often called rocailles) reflect the light even more.
Lustre: the term lustre describes a clear, uniform and shiny finish given to transparent, opal or opaque beads. The well-known term 'pearlised' is given to an opaque lustre bead and opal-lustred beads are also known as 'ceylon'.
Satin: the shade of a satin bead will change depending on how the bead is viewed, for instance, a white satin bead will have quite a distinctive grey shade to one side. The layers or striations are due to the many air bubbles created in its molten stage. The finish has a sheen rather than being too shiny giving it quite an expensive look.
Iridescent: also known as iris, irid, rainbow, Aurora Borealis (AB) and scarab(ee), they are best described as having an 'oil slick'-type finish. Fuming metal salts onto the hot glass to form a permanent bond creates this finish.
Metallic or galvanised: this describes beads given a shiny, metal-like surface coating. Unlike the iridescent finish, this surface is not permanent as it is normally a baked-on paint. When purchasing these types of bead, it is worth checking the manufacturer's recommendations if the finished piece is to be washed or wetted at any time.
Matt metallic: as for metallic, but the finish has a flat rather than a shiny look.
Matt or frosted: this is the name given to a bead with a dull or flat finish. The frosted finish will have a distinctive icy look.

Wire, cottons and thonging

The vast variety of yarn and wire available allows the maker to experiment with colour, texture and thickness like never before. Selecting yarn colours to co-ordinate with your beads will produce a quite different effect from using coloured yarns and wire that contrast with your beads.

WIRE

Working with wire has become increasingly popular over the past few years, with craft wires available in many sizes and a wide range of colours.

When I first started crocheting with wire, I experimented with bits from my toolbox and garden shed: fuse wire, copper picture frame wire and chunky garden wire were all tried with varying degrees of success. Discovering that craft wires were available in a variety of thicknesses and colours enabled me to fine-tune my designs, co-ordinating the coloured wire with wonderful coloured beads.

Wire is measured in millimetres or by the Standard Wire Gauge (swg), and craft wire is available from size 2.00 mm (14 swg) to the fine 0.100 mm (42 swg). The projects in this book are all worked in fine 0.20 mm (36 swg) coloured craft wire, with the exception of the Silver sequin and crystal bracelet project on pages 70–73, which is worked in 0.20 mm silver-plated copper wire. Once confidence is gained with wire, the silver-plated copper wire could be substituted for solid silver wire of the same gauge.

4 PLY COTTON

MERCERISED
CROCHET COTTONS

CROCHET
COTTON

DK COTTON

WIRE

2-MM
THONGING

1-MM
THONGING

COTTONS

Crochet cottons

Commercially produced crochet cottons are available in a wide range of thicknesses, from ultra fine (nos. 100, 80, 70, 60, which are normally available in white only, but can be dyed at home, *see* Dyeing cotton, below) through to 40 and 30, and to the more widely used 20, 10 and 5. The crochet cotton projects in this book are all worked in either no. 5 or no.10 mercerised cotton. The term 'mercerised' is given to the process of treating cotton yarn with an alkali to increase its strength and reception to dye and impart a lustrous silky appearance.

4 ply and DK (double knitting) cottons

When thicker yarn in exciting colours is needed, mercerised crochet cotton becomes almost impossible to source. Fortunately, there are good hand-knitting yarns at reasonable prices.

THONGING

When making a simple chunky crocheted bracelet, thonging makes a great alternative to crochet cottons or knitting yarns. It is available in real leather or waxed cotton, the latter being a great substitute for leather. Cotton thonging is available in a wide range of colours and in 0.5-mm, 1-mm and 2-mm thicknesses. However, if your prefer the real thing, round-leather thonging is best for crochet and it can be found in 1- and 2-mm thicknesses and a few colours in natural shades.

DYEING COTTON

Some cotton yarns are available in a very limited colour palette, but it is not difficult to dye your own white cotton at home. Cold water dyes can be purchased in small tins that are perfect for craft projects. Before the yarn can be dyed, it needs to be prepared into tied 'skeins' as follows.

1 *Wind the yarn to be dyed from the ball over the crux of the hand and around the elbow until the desired amount has been skeined* (left).

2 *Remove the skein from the arm and tie small lengths of yarn around the strands to avoid tangling during the dyeing process. Now follow the dye manufacturer's instructions.*

Findings

The word 'finding' is the generic term to cover all the connectors and closures used to complete jewellery pieces. There are many findings manufactured to connect and finish beaded jewellery and they can be used to great effect to enhance your finished piece. Here is the selection used in this book.

LOBSTER CLASPS

These are used to fasten necklaces and bracelets and are widely available in a variety of finishes and sizes. To fasten, they are normally used in conjunction with a jump ring or necklace tag.

SHEPERD'S CROOK HOOK

A Shepherd's crook hook is normally purchased as a set with a loop to make a fastening or closure and is best used for bracelets and necklaces. The Bali silver hook and loop set used in this book (Purple disc bracelet and earring set, pages 66–69) gives an expensive, ornate finish to the jewellery. Simpler designs are widely available.

ORNATE HOOKS

As well as the Shepherd's hook, hook closures are available in a multitude of shapes, metals and sizes for belts. Most hooks come as a set with a matching jump ring.

BAR AND TOGGLE RING

Available in a multitude of finishes, these are popular for using on loose bracelets and necklaces. They fasten by passing the bar on one end of the work through the ring on the other end and can be either sewn to the piece or connected with jump rings. They are found in a huge range of styles including reproduction antique styles.

CONNECTORS

Also used as bead spacers, these are perfect as fastenings for wider pieces. They work as a transition between the width of the jewellery and the single clasp. They can be purchased individually or in a set with a lobster clasp and chain, making them perfect for chokers that need to fit tight as they produce a fully adjustable fastening.

CHAIN

Adding a length of chain to the back of a choker fastener allows the jewellery to be connected tightly to the neck. Use single link chain, with the links being large enough to close the lobster clasp. A beaded head pin can be added to give a decorative finish to the last link.

BOX CLASPS

Comprised of two pieces, one slotting into the other, they are perfect for bracelets as they are easy and quick to fasten – essential when using one hand! The box clasp illustrated here has a filigree design with two connector rings making it suitable for the wider bracelets.

JUMP RINGS

These are small metal circles of wire used for connecting findings. They are attached by opening and then closing them laterally, rather than pulling them apart as this weakens the metal.

NECKLACE TAGS

These are used in conjunction with a clasp. The smaller hole is attached to the item with a jump ring, and the larger hole becomes the fastener.

EARRING WIRES

These are used for pierced ears and are available in slightly different shapes, the most elegant and popular being the fishhook wire. It is important that sterling silver wires are used to prevent allergic reactions if the earrings are to be given as a gift.

CALOTTES

Also known as knot cups, they act as a transition between the thread and the metal findings. They secure and cover knots and crimp beads at the end of a necklace, bracelet or earring. The knot or crimp bead is placed into the calotte, which is gently squeezed closed with the aid of flat-nose pliers (*see* the Attaching calottes technique on page 26). A jump ring is used to connect the calotte onto a fishhook earring wire or a lobster clasp.

CRIMP BEADS

These are used to secure the crochet wire or thread into a

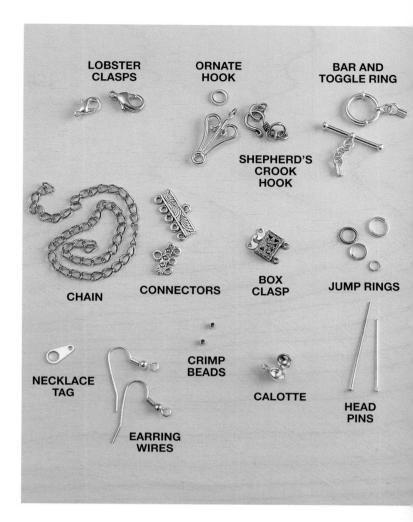

loop. The crimp bead is threaded onto the wire, which is then folded into a loop and the crimp passed over the wire until a desired loop is reached. The crimp bead is squeezed using flat-nose pliers to secure the loop. For extra strength, two crimp beads can be used for each loop.

HEAD PINS

A head pin is a straight wire with a small perpendicular disc at one end. Head pins are used for stringing beads, with the pinhead acting as a stopper and the other end bent into a loop to attach to a jump ring or another finding.

If a number of pieces of jewellery are planned, it is worth buying the findings in large quantities as it is certainly more cost effective. Alternatively, some companies sell variety packs containing an assortment of jump rings and closures.

Equipment

The advantage of crochet work is that you can get started with a small investment in a couple of hooks and some pins. Working with wire adds a few more tools to the workbox, which fortunately won't break the bank and can be used for other jewellery projects.

CROCHET HOOKS

Crochet hooks can be made from steel, aluminium, plastic, wood, bamboo or bone (the latter are usually antique and can be occasionally found in second-hand shops and antique fairs). Any of these are suitable for crocheting with cottons, although the metal hooks are best for wirework. Very fat hooks are normally made of plastic, but wood and bamboo hooks are becoming increasingly popular and, as a result, more outlets are stocking them.

Sizes are stamped or printed onto hooks and define the diameter of the hook in millimetres (metric). Older (English) hooks have numbers, whereas numbers and letters define American hook sizes. The chart below should help you to convert hook sizes.

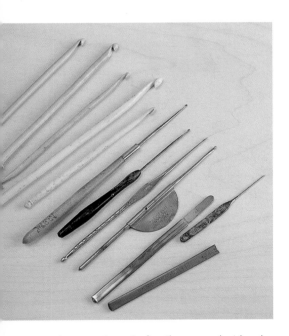

An assortment of antique crochet hooks illustrating the different handle grips and materials used.

CROCHET HOOK SIZE

Metric	English	USA
0.60 mm	6	14
0.75 mm	5	12
1.00 mm	4	10
1.25 mm	3	9/8
1.50 mm	2½	7/6
1.75 mm	2	5
2.00 mm	1 steel / 14 aluminium	1 steel / B aluminium
2.25 mm		13
2.50 mm	2/0 steel / 12 aluminium	2/0 steel / C aluminium
3.00 mm	11	–
3.25 mm	10	3/0 / D
3.50 mm	9	4/0 / E
3.75 mm	–	5/0 / F
4.00 mm	8	6/0 / G
4.50 mm	7	7
5.00 mm	6	8/0 / H
5.50 mm	5	9/0 / I
6.00 mm	4	10/0 / J
6.50 mm	3	10½ / K
7.00 mm	2	–
8.00 mm	0	11/0 / L
9.00 mm	00	13/0 / M
10.00 mm	000	15/0 / N
15.00 mm	–	16/0 / P
16.00 mm	–	Q
19.00 mm	–	S

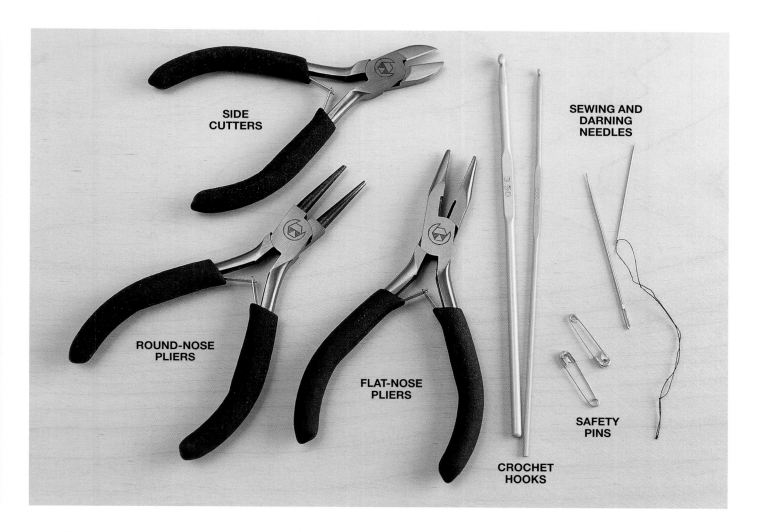

SIDE CUTTERS

ROUND-NOSE PLIERS

FLAT-NOSE PLIERS

CROCHET HOOKS

SEWING AND DARNING NEEDLES

SAFETY PINS

ROUND-NOSE PLIERS

To avoid the surface of the wire being spoiled, the pliers used for wirework jewellery do not have teeth like the conventional types. Round-nose pliers are used for gripping and bending wire – they have round, tight jaws that taper to a point.

FLAT-NOSE PLIERS

Flat-nose pliers have tapered jaws that have a flat inside edge. They are used for opening and closing jump rings and for squeezing crimp beads. Lightweight, smooth-jawed pliers avoid damage to the wire. Flat-nose pliers also come with an angled head. It is useful to use a pair of each to attach small jump rings to connectors.

SIDE CUTTERS

Also known as flush cutters, the cutting end has a flat side and an angled side. The flat side is positioned against the work for a straight close cut. The blade is very sharp to avoid burring (or marking) the metal. Choose a small, lightweight pair for jewellery making.

SEWING AND DARNING NEEDLES

It is useful to have a selection of various sized sewing and darning needles for fastening and neatening off. Small-eyed sewing needles are used for threading seed beads onto crochet cotton and larger darning needles are used for neatening tail ends and attaching findings.

SAFETY PINS

Keep a good selection of small safety pins to hand – they are invaluable for use as markers or for holding a loop for storing work in progress.

Techniques

Learning just a few basic stitches will open up a whole new and useful skill set. Crochet is ideal for making jewellery, garments and home furnishings and is definitely the craft to take up if you like quick results.

Holding the hook and yarn

HOLDING THE HOOK

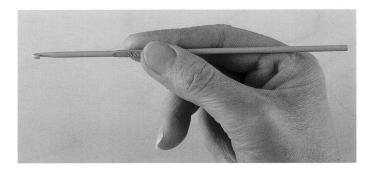

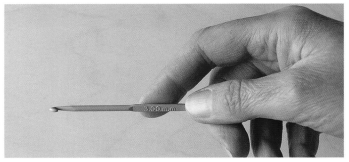

The pencil grip is certainly the more elegant hold – probably favoured by 'ladies-that-lunch' crochet groups

The over hand grip is a firmer hold and it could be likened to the way a child first learns to hold a knife – a bit clumsy, but done with purpose (my preferred method).

HOLDING THE YARN

Right-handed crochet The hook is held and controlled in the right hand and the left hand controls the yarn supply and holds the work. There are two popular ways of holding the yarn.

Either way, to maintain a slight tension on the yarn either continue to wrap the yarn round the little finger or grip loosely with the two smallest fingers.

Control the yarn by looping over the left hand index finger and hold the work just under the hook between the middle finger and thumb.

Control the yarn by looping over the middle finger and hold the work just under the hook between the index finger and thumb

Left-handed crochet Stand the book next to a mirror and work from the pictures in mirror image. Better still, if you have a

crocheting friend, ask them to sit in front of a mirror whilst they work; stand behind and watch the techniques in mirror image.

Crochet stitches

Crochet stitches are the same whether the chosen yarn is wire, cotton or thonging. The following section outlines all the basic stitches that are used in the book so follow these steps to help get you started. Where more complicated stitches are used in a project, they have been detailed under 'Special instructions' within the pattern for easy reference.

SLIPKNOT

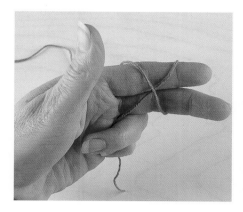

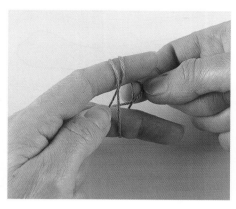

1 *Leaving enough tail end for attaching the findings, place the end of the yarn in the palm of the hand and hold in place with the bottom two fingers. Straighten out the index and middle fingers and wind the yarn over and around these fingers, crossing the yarn at the front of the fingers.*

2 *Still holding the tail end in place, make a scissors with the top two fingers and push a loop through from the back.*

3 *Take the fingers out of the loop and pull the loop and the tail end gently until a knot is formed. The loop can be made smaller by pulling the yarn from the spool end.*

CHAIN STITCH (ch)

SLIP STITCH (sl.st)

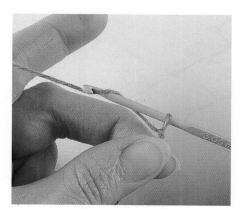

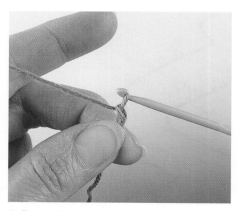

1 *Place the slipknot onto the hook and adjust to tension. Wrap the yarn over the hook in an anti-clockwise direction.*

2 *Draw the yarn through to form a new loop (this must be done without tightening the previous loop). Continue to form loops in the same way until required length of chain is formed.*

1 *Used to join circles, in decreasing and to move across work. Insert the hook into the stitch, wrap the yarn over the hook and draw the yarn through the work and the loop in one movement.*

BEAD CHAIN STITCH (Bch)

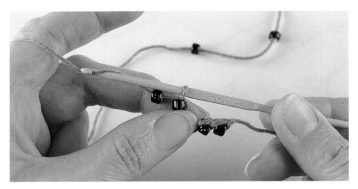 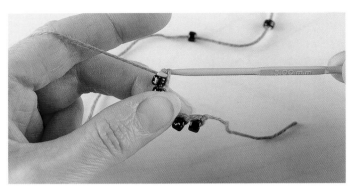

1 *Place the slipknot onto the hook and adjust to tension. Slide a bead next to the loop on the hook and wrap the yarn over the hook.*

2 *Draw the yarn through to form a new loop securing the bead in the first chain. Continue to form loops in the same way until the required length of bead chain is formed.*

DOUBLE CROCHET (dc)

1 *Insert the hook into the next stitch (or the second chain from hook for foundation row) and wrap the yarn over the hook.*

2 *Draw the yarn through the work to form a second loop on the hook.*

3 *Wrap the yarn over the hook and draw the yarn through both loops on the hook.*

BEAD DOUBLE CROCHET (Bdc)

1 *Insert the hook into the next stitch (or the second chain from hook for foundation row). Slide a bead next to the loop on the hook and wrap the yarn over hook.*

2 *Draw the yarn through the work to form a second loop on the hook. The bead will sit to the back of the work, which will become the right side.*

3 *Wrap the yarn over the hook and draw the yarn through both loops on the hook.*

TREBLE CROCHET (tr)

1 *Wrap the yarn over the hook and insert the hook into the next stitch (or the fourth chain from hook for the foundation row).*

2 *Wrap the yarn over the hook and draw the yarn through the work to form a third loop on the hook.*

3 *Wrap the yarn over the hook and draw the yarn through the first two loops on the hook.*

4 *Wrap again, drawing through the last two loops on the hook.*

BEAD TREBLE CROCHET (Btr)

 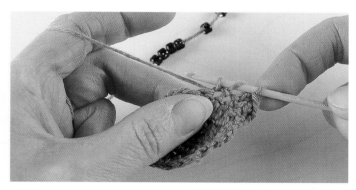

1 *Wrap the yarn over the hook and insert the hook into the next stitch (or the fourth chain from hook for the foundation row).*

2 *Wrap the yarn over the hook and draw the yarn through the work to form a third loop on the hook.*

 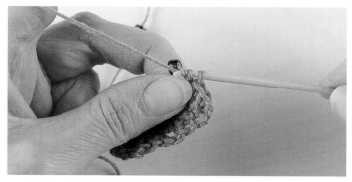

3 *Slide a bead next to the loop on the hook, yarn over the hook and draw the yarn through the first two loops on the hook.*

4 *Wrap again, drawing through the remaining two loops on the hook. The bead will sit to the back of the work, which will become the right side.*

SHELL (sh)

Working more than one stitch into the same place to create a fan effect produces shell stitches. In the Black jet chevron choker project on pages 82–85, shell stitches are worked in conjunction with clusters to produce a chevron pattern. Shells are most commonly worked with treble stitches as follows:

1 *Work a treble into a stitch. Continue to create more trebles into the same stitch to create a fan effect of the desired size.*

CLUSTERS

Clusters are worked by starting stitches in different places, temporarily leaving the last loop on the hook. All the loops are then drawn together at the top to create a single stitch.

Use either as a decorative stitch or as a method for decreasing to add shape to a piece. Special instructions for adding beads to clusters can be found on page 82.

TREBLE CLUSTER OVER THREE STITCHES (Tr3tog)

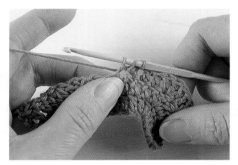

1 * *Wrap the yarn over the hook and insert the hook into the next stitch.*

2 *Wrap the yarn over the hook and draw the yarn through the work to form another loop on the hook.*

3 *Yarn over hook, draw through two loops.*

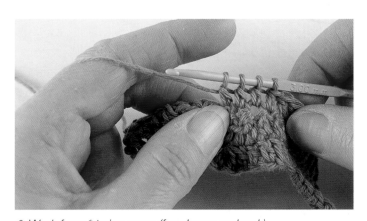

4 *Work from * twice more (four loops on hook).*

5 *Yarn over hook, draw through all loops.*

TREBLE CLUSTER OVER TWO STITCHES (Tr2tog)

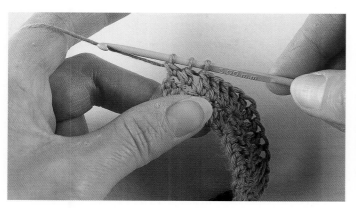

1 *As opposite but work from * twice (three loops on hook).*

2 *Yarn over hook, draw through all loops on hook.*

Reading and understanding crochet patterns

There is some basic crochet instruction jargon that should be understood before undertaking a project and it is always advisable to read the pattern through carefully before starting.

FOUNDATION ROW

This is the first row worked into the length of base chain. It is really important to get this row right as it sets the stitches for the rest of the pattern.

TURNING CHAIN

To produce an even edge to a sample, turning chains are used at the beginning of each row. The number of chains worked is dependent on the stitches being used at the beginning of the row – normally one chain for a double crochet and three chains for a treble crochet.

BRACKETS ([ ]) AND ASTERISKS (*)

Brackets and asterisks are used when a set of instructions has repetition. Instructions are put in brackets followed by a number, which denotes how many times the instructions should be worked. An example of the use of brackets is as follows:

[1 bugle, 1 seed, 1 sequin, 1 seed] 3 times.
This instruction means work the sequence three times, giving twelve beads in total.

Asterisks are used for repeating a whole sequence. For example:

Neckband Row 1: 1 Bdc into first dc, * 1 dc, 1 Bdc, rep from * to end, 1 ch turn.

The repeat is always started from the * and not from the beginning of the row and in this example, the sequence will finish at the end of the row. Sometimes there will be a further instruction to complete the row after the last repeat. It is important that the pattern is completed to the end of the row.

Working with wire

A 0.20-mm wire is a good gauge for crochet; the fineness allows it to be treated like fine crochet cotton. Very fine seed beads can be threaded easily and used in the designs and it retains a lightweight softness in the finished pieces. Crochet stitches have a tendency to become very hard and uncontrollable when worked too tightly, the fine gauge wire prevents the stitches from becoming too tight and distorted and it is kinder on the hands. To prevent tangling and snagging, buy the wire on small plastic spools (rather than coils) to allow it to run freely as you crochet.

Care should always be taken when working with wire. The advantage of the fine gauge wire is that it is very delicate and unlikely to cause injury. But it is advisable to wear protective eyewear when cutting wire and always dispose of the spare tail ends carefully.

Crocheting with beads

All the projects in this book require the beads to be strung onto the yarn before the crocheting is started. Follow the bead set-up instructions for each project and once the beads are threaded, make a slipknot to prevent the beads sliding back off.

THREADING BEADS ONTO WIRE

The beauty of working with fine wire is that the beads can be threaded straight onto the wire without the use of additional aids.

1 *Pour the beads into a shallow dish, preferably one that doesn't have ridges in which small seed beads can get trapped. Make a very slight bend in the end of the wire and push the wire gently through the beads – the seed beads will just pop onto the wire!*

THREADING BEADS ONTO CROCHET COTTON

As cotton is less rigid than wire, threading beads onto cotton yarns requires the use of sewing needles. The size of the needle used will be dependent on the thickness of the cotton yarn and the size of the beads.

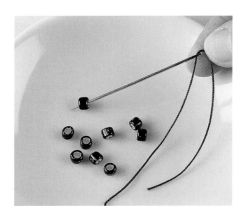

1 *If the beads used have large holes, thread the cotton straight onto a large-eye knitter's sewing needle to string the correct amount of beads to complete the project.*

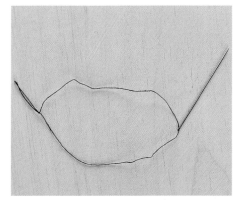

2 *When threading seed beads and bugle beads, thread a small amount (about 10 cm/4 in) of strong sewing thread into a small-eyed sewing needle and tie the ends into a knot to make a loop. Now pass the end of the crochet cotton into the loop and draw through about 3 cm (1¼ in).*

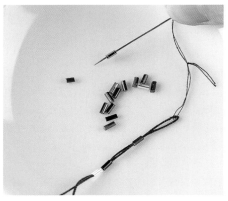

3 *The sewing needle can be now used to pick up the fine beads and each bead can be pulled through the double thickness of crochet cotton until it reaches the single thread.*

Finishing off with wire

One of the advantages of working with wire is that it doesn't easily unravel when you come to finish off a piece of work.

Unfortunately, the disadvantage is that it's less easy to unpick stitches once the last stitch is secured.

TO FINISH THE LAST STITCH

When the pattern is completed, leave a tail end and cut the wire. Pass the end through the last loop and pull to fasten off. This tail end can be used for sewing findings, joining the seam for a ring or it can be darned into the work to neaten off.

SEWING ON FINDINGS

Always bear in mind that jump rings and ear wires have tiny gaps that will allow a single thread of wire to escape, therefore when attaching findings, make four to five over-sew stitches to secure.

DARNING OFF TAIL ENDS

To neaten off tail ends, thread the tail end onto a large-eyed sewing needle and weave through the last row of the work. Threading the wire through any beads on the way will help to secure. Continue until all the ends are darned. Trim close to the work with side cutters.

Finishing off with cotton

A piece crocheted in cotton remains unstable until the last stitch is secured. Unlike wire, this makes the cotton easy to unravel if

corrections need to be made to the pattern. Cotton is less likely to spoil if it is unpicked soon after it has been crocheted.

TO FINISH THE LAST STITCH

When the pattern is completed, leave a tail end and cut the yarn. Pass the end through the last loop and pull to fasten off. This tail end can be used for sewing findings, joining seams or it can be darned into the work to neaten off.

SEWING ON FINDINGS

Over-sew as with the wire, but bear in mind that cotton is a lot thicker, therefore will not require as many stitches. Thicker yarn can be split for sewing the small connector holes of some of the finer findings, such as filigree clasps.

DARNING OFF TAIL ENDS

It is tempting to knot the two ends of the cotton together; not only does this create an unsightly lump, but it may work loose over time. Neaten off one tail end at a time and weave in different directions to avoid excess thickness. Also splitting the back of the crochet stitches makes the darn more secure.

SEWING SEAMS WITH COTTON OR WIRE

The two ring projects on pages 77 and 86–88 require that the two ends of the piece are joined to make a circle. Thread up one of the tail ends onto a large-eyed sewing needle and slip stitch to create a flat seam.

JOINING A NEW LENGTH OF COTTON OR WIRE

Occasionally, it may be necessary to join in a new ball of yarn or wire to finish a project or to change colour. This is best done at the beginning of a row to allow the tail ends to be darned into a seam or to be used to attach findings. The new yarn should be joined as follows:

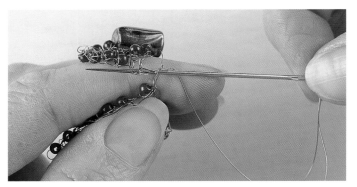

Gently fold the ring around your index finger with the ends to be sewn clearly visible. Pick up the first stitch from one edge of the ring, repeat for the corresponding stitch on the opposite edge. Continue to slip stitch each until the seam is complete.

1 *Work until the last two loops of the last stitch in the row are left on the hook.*

2 *Leave a 4 cm (1½ in) tail end on the new yarn and draw through the two loops to finish the stitch, turn and continue the next row as set.*

Finishing off with findings

The way the findings are attached to the piece should be considered carefully as part of the overall design and finish of the project. The right choice of findings will greatly enhance a piece of jewellery giving it a really professional look.

ATTACHING JUMP RINGS WITH PLIERS

Jump rings should be attached carefully by opening and closing them laterally rather than pulling them apart, which will distort the shape.

ATTACHING CALOTTES

Think of a calotte as a tiny hinged box for hiding unsightly tail ends. A calotte will add a touch of professionalism to your work.

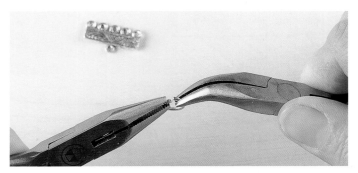

A couple of pairs of lightweight, flat-nose pliers are best used for the job. Here, one of the pairs has an angled head.

Make a secure knot out of the tail ends, trim the excess and place into one half of the calotte. There is a small nick in the bottom edge of the calotte to accommodate the wire or cotton from the finished piece. When the thread is lined up with the nick, carefully close the calotte, firstly pinching with your fingers then squeezing to secure with flat-nose pliers.

MAKING AN ADJUSTABLE CHOKER CLASP

Adjustable choker clasps can be bought in ready-made sets, but they are costly and are limited in size and finishes. They are simple to make as follows:

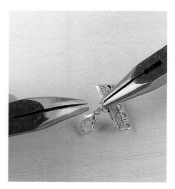 

1 *Attach a lobster clasp to the single hole of a transition connector with a jump ring.*

2 *To the single hole of a second transition connector, attach an 8 cm (3¼ in) length of chain using a 7-cm (2½-in) jump ring.*

MAKING A BEADED HEAD PIN

The raw chain-end of the choker clasp can be finished by adding a beaded head pin as follows:

1 *Thread a few beads onto a head pin.*

2 *Using round-nose pliers, bend the tip of the head pin to form a loop. Thread the loop through the end link of the chain before closing securely.*

Abbreviations

Crochet patterns are filled with abbreviations to make printed instructions shorter in length. Fortunately, abbreviations tend to be standard so it is worth familiarising yourself with them.

Keep a copy of the list below to have close at hand until you are more experienced and before you know it, you will be reading and understanding them like a second language!

Ch	Chain	MSK	Main Solomon's knot
Bch	Bead chain	Sl.st	Slip stitch
Dc	Double crochet	Rep.	Repeat
Bdc	Bead double crochet	G	Grams
Tr	Treble	Mm	Millimetre
Btr	Bead treble	Cm	Centimetre
Btr2	Bead treble, inserting bead before last yoh	M	Metre
YOH	Yarn over hook	In	Inch
Tr2 tog	Treble 2 together (cluster)	Col.	Colour
Tr3 tog	Treble 3 together (cluster)	Approx.	Approximately
Btr3 tog	Bead cluster	[]	Repeat brackets
Sh	Shell	* to *	Repeat asterisks
Bsh	Bead shell	RS	Right side
ESK	End Solomon's knot	WS	Wrong side
BESK	End Bead Solomon's knot		

THE PROJECTS

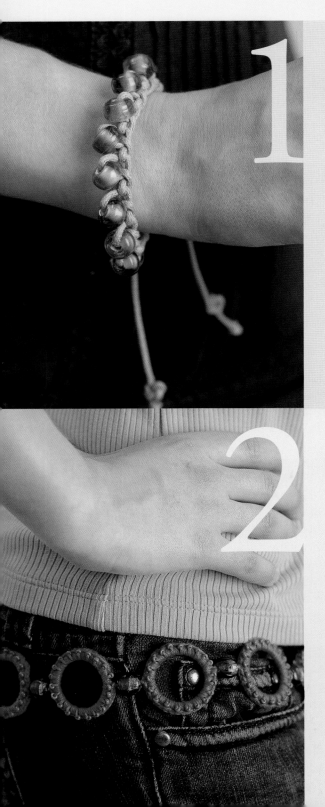

1 getting you started

This section has been designed for those who are completely new to crochet and for those inexperienced in working with beads or wire. These simple projects will help the beginner get started and quickly produce fruits from their labour. There is, of course, no reason why the pieces can't be worked by the most experienced crocheters.

2 working with cotton

There are certain crochet bead projects that lend themselves better to traditional crochet cottons and 4 ply cottons. Beginners may find that the cotton projects in this section are easier to work than some of the wire designs. The designs are ordered with the simplest patterns first.

3 using sequins and discs

Adding sequins and discs to crochet produces some wonderful sparkly effects. In each design in this section the sequins or discs have been crocheted in pairs or in sets of three to add more movement to the finished pieces.

4 for the more experienced

This section introduces some interesting crochet stitch patterns to the projects that take a little more skill and concentration to complete. Again the projects have been ordered with the simplest project first.

Glass bead wristband

This simple wristband is easily achievable in a couple of hours and is a perfect project for a complete beginner. The combination of sturdy waxed cotton thonging and stunning glass beads create a modern Bohemian wristband. The knotted drawstring fastening gives a unisex look and allows the band to fit any size wrist, but beads can be easily added or taken away to adjust the size.

★ ☆ ☆ **SKILL LEVEL** EASY

• *Captioned step-by-step pictures on page 32.*

HOT TIP
Experiment with different styles of beads and types of thonging. Try plastic thonging with fun plastic beads for the children or even leather or twine with wooden or bone beads for a more urban look

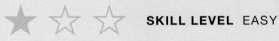

The wristband

MATERIALS
- 1 m (39 in) of 2.00 mm natural waxed cotton thonging
- 6 x 10 mm aqua glass pony beads
- 5 x 10 mm olive glass pony beads
- 3.50 mm hook

FINISHED SIZE
Beaded length: 13 cm (5⅛ in)
Total length: 35 cm (13¾ in)

BEAD SET UP
Starting and finishing with aqua, alternate with olive until 11 beads are threaded onto the cotton thonging.

WRISTBAND
Leaving an end of approx. 20 cm (8 in), make a slipknot.
Using 3.50 mm hook, work 1 Bch, * 1 ch, 1 Bch, rep from * until all the beads are used.
Break yarn, leaving an end of 15 cm (6 in). Fasten off.

FINISHING
Make drawstring fastening: Using the length of yarn at the beginning of the work and leaving a 2.5 cm (1 in) space from the first bead, make 2 half hitch knots over the remaining length of yarn. Tie double knots in the ends of each tail and trim excess close to knot to finish.

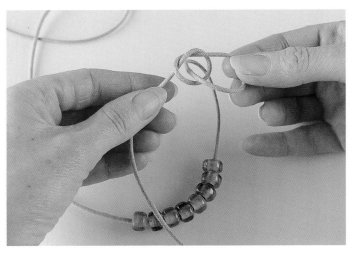

1 *Making a slip knot.*

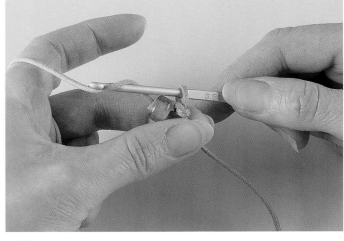

2 *Working a bead chain (Bch).*

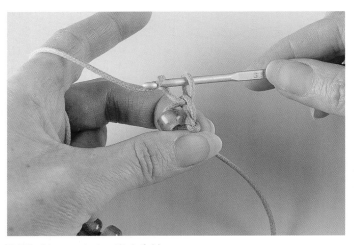

3 *Working a chain stitch (ch).*

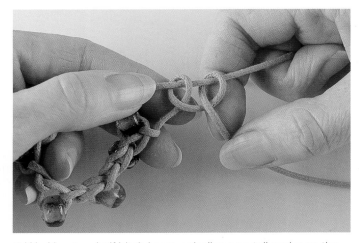

4 *Working two half hitch knots; winding one tail end over the other, bringing the tail to the front after the second wind.*

5 *Tying double knots in the end of each tail.*

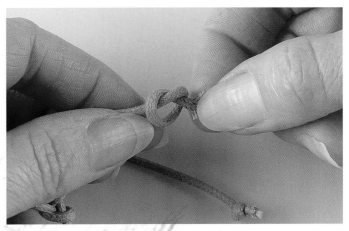

Multi-string bugle bead necklace

Many bead retailers sell bugle beads in mixed bags of colours. This Candy Mix has been teamed with a rich pink wire to wonderful effect. The design has seven strings of beaded chains, but more can be added easily to suit your taste. The wires are brought together at each end with a pretty glass bead and the necklace is topped off with gold findings.

 **SKILL LEVEL** EASY

• *Captioned step-by-step pictures on page 34.*

HOT TIP
To allow the beads to lie flat, make sure each chain is drawn to the length of the bead. Allow a 7 cm (2¾ in) tail at each end to join to the findings.

The necklace

MATERIALS
- Small spool of 0.20 mm (36 swg) pink wire
- Approx. 12 g of 5 mm candy mix silver-lined bugle beads
- 2 x 10 mm cerise glass beads
- 1.25 mm hook
- 2 x 7 mm gold jump rings
- Large gold lobster clasp
- Large gold necklace tag, or 7 mm gold jump ring

FINISHED SIZE
Length (including findings): 44 cm (17¼ in) at its shortest length

BEAD SET UP
Thread between 58 and 70 bugle beads onto the wire for each length of chain.

NECKLACE
Work approx. 38 cm (15 in) length of chain, bringing in a bugle bead for each chain stitch. Cut wire, leaving a 7 cm (2¾ in) tail. Continue to work 6 more chain lengths in the same way, varying each length by approx. 1 cm (½ in).

FINISHING
Attach a 7 mm jump ring to the lobster clasp and close to secure. Arrange the lengths of chain in size order. Twist the tails of one end together and thread through the glass bead, the jump ring and back through the bead. Wind the tails a few times around the base of the bead to secure. Cut close and repeat for the other end, attaching a necklace tag or jump ring in place of the lobster clasp.

1 *Using wire end, threading on enough beads for each length of chain.*

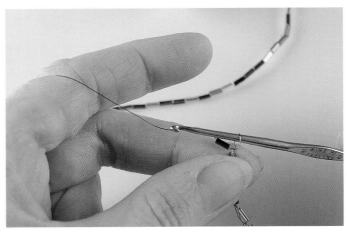

2 *Working bead chain (Bch) until all the beads are finished.*

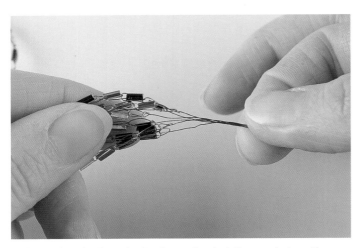

3 *Arranging the lengths in size order, twisting ends together.*

4 *Threading tails through the glass bead, the jump ring and back through the bead.*

5 *Winding the tails around the base of the bead.*

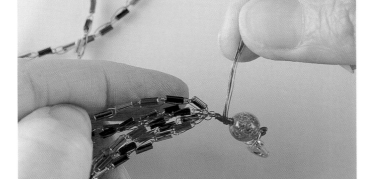

Glass bead and wire necklace and earring set

This is a good project for someone attempting crochet with wire for the first time. It is a very simple project made special with the use of the stunning glass beads. The colours of the beads are beautifully enhanced with the use of the fine black wire.

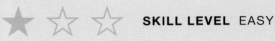

SKILL LEVEL EASY

• *Captioned step-by-step pictures on pages 38–39.*

HOT TIP

The success of this piece is dependent on beautifully even chain stitches. Practise on a spare length of wire before embarking on this project.

The necklace

MATERIALS FOR NECKLACE

- Small spool of 0.20 mm (36 swg) black wire
- 4 silver-lined bicoloured (lime/lilac) 12 mm glass discs
- 3 silver-lined bicoloured (turquoise/lime) 12 mm glass discs
- Six 8 x 6 mm turquoise frosted glass drop beads
- 3.50 mm hook
- Large pewter lobster clasp
- Large pewter necklace tag
- 2 gold crimp beads

FINISHED SIZE

Length (including findings): 43 cm (17 in)

BEAD SET UP

Thread onto the wire * 1 lime/lilac, 1 glass frosted, 1 turquoise/lime, 1 glass frosted, rep from * twice more, 1 lime/lilac.

NECKLACE

Using 3.50 mm hook, make 20 ch (measuring approx. 12 cm/5 in), 1 Bch, * 1 ch, 1 Bch, rep from * until all 13 beads have been worked, 20 ch.

Leaving an 8 cm (3¼ in) tail, cut wire and fasten off.

FINISHING

Thread one tail end through a crimp bead, the lobster clasp and back through the crimp bead. Pull to within 5 mm (¼ in) of first chain stitch and squeeze crimp bead to secure. Wind the tail a few times around the base of the crimp bead and trim close to finish. Repeat for other end, joining onto the necklace tag instead of the lobster clasp.

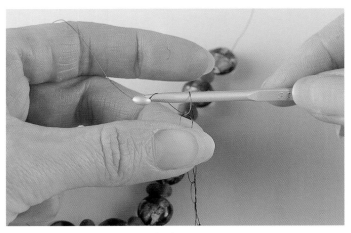

1 *Making 20 chain stitches (ch).*

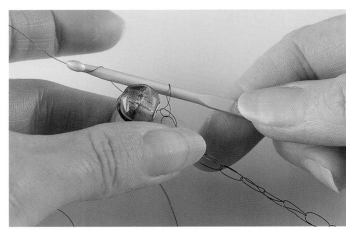

2 *Working a bead chain (Bch) using a glass disc.*

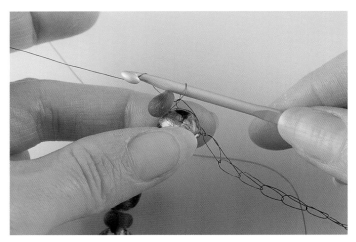

3 *Working a bead chain (Bch) using a frosted drop bead.*

4 *Threading the tail end through the crimp bead, lobster clasp and back through the crimp bead.*

5 *Winding the tail end around the base of the crimp bead.*

The earrings

MATERIALS FOR EARRINGS

- Small spool of 0.20 mm (36 swg) black wire
- 4 silver-lined bicoloured (lime/lilac) 12 mm glass discs
- 2 silver-lined bicoloured (turquoise/lime) 12 mm glass discs
- Six 8 x 6 mm turquoise frosted glass drop beads
- 3.50 mm hook
- 2 gold fishhook earring wires
- 2 gold calottes
- 2 x 5 mm gold jump rings

FINISHED SIZE

Length: 8 cm (3¼ in) to bend of fishhook

BEAD SET UP

Thread onto the wire 1 lime/lilac, 1 glass frosted, 1 turquoise/lime, 1 glass frosted, 1 lime/lilac, 1 glass frosted.

EARRING

Using 3.50 mm hook, work * 1 ch, 1 Bch, rep from * four times more, 1 ch, bring up last frosted bead and slip stitch into first chain to make a loop. Make a second earring to match.

FINISHING

Twist the wires together to make a tight knot. Place the knot into a calotte and squeeze to close. Join the calotte to a fishhook earring wire with a 5 mm jump ring.

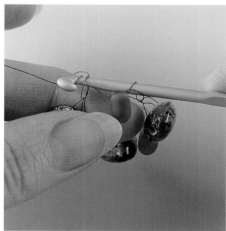

1 Slip stitching (sl.st) into first chain to make a loop.

2 Placing the knot into the calotte, lining up the wire with the nick in the calotte.

Hearts choker and earring set

The prettiest combination of delicate red glass hearts and gold transparent seed beads makes this set tick all the right boxes. Easily achievable in an evening by a complete beginner and making it won't break the bank.

★ ☆ ☆ **SKILL LEVEL** EASY

• Captioned step-by-step pictures on pages 42–43.

HOT TIP

Make sure that the brass wires of the heart pendants are tightly closed before use.

SPECIAL INSTRUCTIONS

Bch – Bead chain Bring up 3 seed beads for each chain. Make the Bch the same tension as a normal chain – in this way the gold seed beads will form small loops.

HBch – Heart Bead chain Bring up 1 Heart pendant for each chain.

The choker

MATERIALS FOR CHOKER

- Small spool of 0.20 mm (36 swg) light gold wire
- 12 x 6 mm red glass hearts with brass loops
- 78 size 8/0 silver-lined gold transparent seed beads
- 2.00 mm hook
- 2 gold calottes
- 2 gold crimp beads
- 2 x 5 mm gold jump rings
- Medium gold lobster clasp
- 7 mm gold jump ring

FINISHED SIZE

Length (including findings): 36 cm (14 in)

BEAD SET UP

Thread onto the wire 6 seed, * 1 heart, 6 seed, rep from * until 12 hearts are threaded, ending 6 seed.

CHOKER

Using 2.00 mm hook, make 1 ch, 1 Bch, 1 ch, 1 Bch, * 1 ch, 1 HBch, 1 ch, 1 Bch, 1 ch, 1 Bch, rep from * until all beads are worked. Leaving an 8 cm (3¼ in) tail, cut wire and fasten off.

FINISHING

Thread wire end into a crimp bead, squeeze and knot to secure. Place the knotted end into a calotte and close. Join to the lobster clasp with a 5 mm jump ring. Repeat for other end, joining the calotte to the 7 mm jump ring with a 5 mm jump ring.

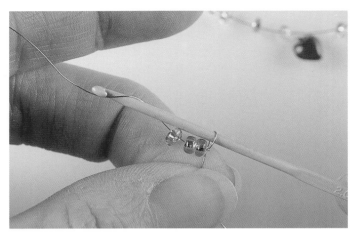

1 *Working a bead chain (Bch) using 3 seed beads.*

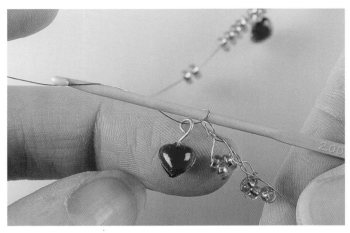

2 *Bringing up a heart bead and working a HBch.*

3 *Knotting wire onto the crimp bead and placing into a calotte.*

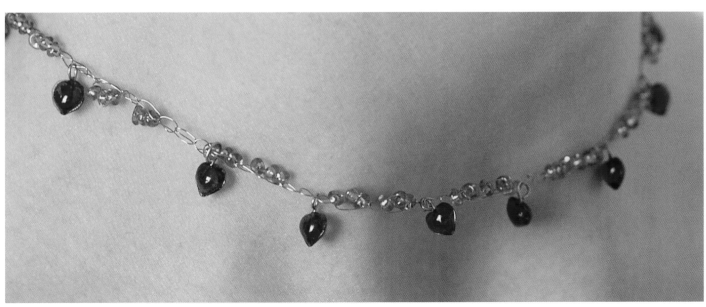

The earrings

MATERIALS FOR EARRINGS

- Small spool of 0.20 mm (36 swg) light gold wire
- 6 x 6 mm red glass hearts with brass loops
- 42 size 8/0 silver-lined gold transparent seed beads
- 2.00 mm hook
- 2 gold calottes
- 2 gold crimp beads
- 2 x 5 mm gold jump ring
- 2 gold fishhook earring wires

FINISHED SIZE

Length: 8 cm (3¼ in) to bend of fishhook

BEAD SET UP

Thread onto the wire * 6 seed, 1 heart, rep from * twice more, 3 seed.

EARRING

Using 2.00 mm hook, make 1 ch, 1 Bch, * 1 ch, 1 HBch, 1 ch, 1 Bch, 1 ch, 1 Bch, rep from * once more, 1ch, 1 Hbch, 1 ch, 1 Bch, 1 ch, sl.st into first ch to make a ring, 1 Bch.
Leaving an 8 cm (3¼ in) tail, cut wire and fasten off.
Make a second earring to match.

FINISHING

Twist wire ends together and thread through a crimp bead. Squeeze crimp bead to secure the wires and trim close. Place crimp bead in a calotte and close to cover crimp bead.

Join a fishhook earring wire to the calotte with a 5 mm jump ring.

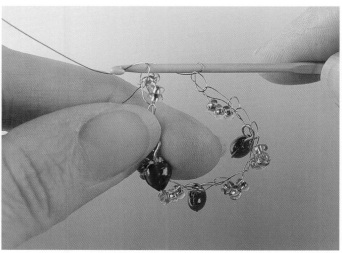

1 *Slip stitching (sl.st) into first chain to make a ring.*

2 *Bringing up 3 seed beads and working a bead chain (Bch) before attaching the calotte.*

Blue pendants necklace and earring set

The unusual colour combination and bead selection make this set really striking. Blue faceted glass is framed in pewter to form interesting pendants that contrast beautifully with the brilliant cerise glass beads and tiny scarab seed beads. These very simple patterns are easily achievable in an evening.

★ ☆ ☆   **SKILL LEVEL** EASY

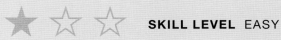

• Captioned step-by-step pictures on page 46.

HOT TIP

The success of this piece is dependent on beautifully even chain and beaded chain stitches. Practise on a spare length of wire before embarking on the main projects.

SPECIAL INSTRUCTIONS

The cerise glass beads and the blue glass pendants are crocheted singularly whilst the seed beads are crocheted in pairs throughout. Leave 8 cm (3¼ in) tail ends for sewing findings.

The necklace

MATERIALS FOR NECKLACE

- Small spool of 0.20 mm (36 swg) black wire
- Five 18 x 8 mm metal pendants with faceted blue glass centre
- 6 x 10 mm cerise glass beads
- 60 size 10/0 purple scarab seed beads
- 2.00 mm hook
- Medium pewter lobster clasp
- Medium pewter necklace tag
- Sewing needle

FINISHED SIZE

Length (including findings): 40 cm (15¾ in)

BEAD SET UP

Thread onto the wire 20 seed, * 1 cerise, 2 seed, 1 glass pendant, 2 seed, rep from * 4 times more, 1 cerise, 20 seed.

NECKLACE

Using 2.00 mm hook and following the special instructions, make 1 ch, * 1 Bch, 1 ch, rep from * until all the beads are worked.
Leaving an 8 cm (3¼ in) tail, cut wire and fasten off.

FINISHING

Using one of the tail wires, sew one of the end chains onto the connector ring of the lobster clasp. Repeat for the other end, attaching the necklace tag. Neaten off and trim the tail ends close to the work.

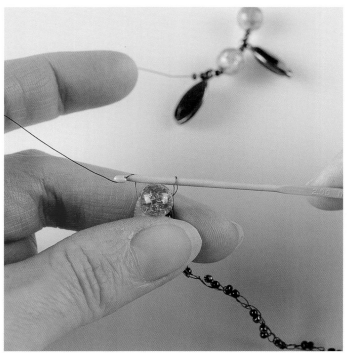

1 *Working a bead chain (Bch) using a cerise glass bead.*

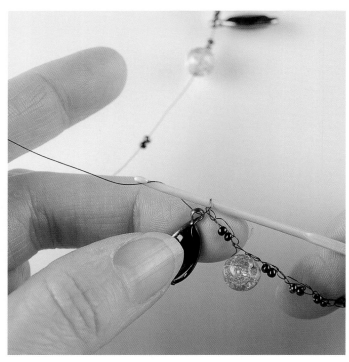

2 *Working a bead chain (Bch) using a blue glass pendant.*

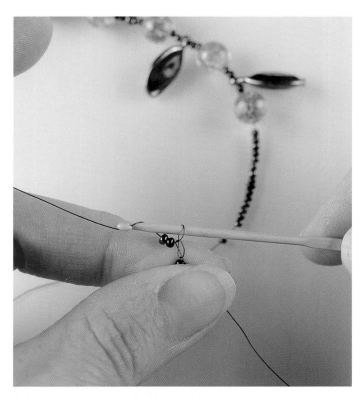

3 *Working a bead chain (Bch) using 2 seed beads.*

4 *Earring: slip stitching (sl.st) into first chain to form a ring.*

The earrings

MATERIALS FOR EARRINGS

- Small spool of 0.20 mm (36 swg) black wire
- Two 18 x 8 mm metal pendants with faceted blue glass centre
- 4 x 10 mm cerise glass beads
- 24 size 10/0 purple scarab seed beads
- 2.00 mm hook
- 2 x 5mm silver jump rings
- 2 silver fishhook earring wires
- Sewing needle

FINISHED SIZE

Length: 8 cm (3¼ in) to bend of fishhook

BEAD SET UP

Thread onto the wire 4 seed, 1 cerise, 2 seed, 1 glass pendant, 2 seed, 1 cerise, 4 seed.

EARRING

Using 2.00 mm hook and following the special instructions, make 1 ch, * 1 Bch, 1 ch, rep from * until all the beads are worked, sl.st into first ch.
Leaving an 8 cm (3¼ in) tail, cut wire and fasten off.
Make a second earring to match.

FINISHING

Join a jump ring to a fishhook earring wire. Twist together the two tail wires and sew onto the jump ring. Repeat for the other earring. Neaten off and trim the tail ends close to the work.

Beaded bands for neck, wrist and ankle

A simple crochet bead pattern has been used to create bands of varying widths suitable for the neck, wrist and ankle. The clasps have been selected according to the weight and width of each band. Variations can be made by working a one-bead row neckband or a three-bead row wrist or ankle band.

★ ☆ ☆ **SKILL LEVEL** EASY

• Captioned step-by-step pictures on page 50.

HOT TIP

When working the bead rows, keep checking the right side of work to make sure that the beads are being crocheted in the right place. The bead positions should alternate on every wrong side row. Try substituting the glass beads for wooden beads or plastic pony beads to create different looks.

The neckband

MATERIALS FOR NECKBAND

- 50 g ball Coats Aida 5 100% crochet cotton (col. 926 Cream)
- 108 size 5/0 pink pearlised seed beads
- 2.00 mm hook
- Medium gold lobster clasp
- 5 mm gold jump ring
- 7 mm gold jump ring
- 2 gold end connectors (3 holes on one side and 1 hole on the other)
- 8 cm (3¼ in) length of gold chain
- Sewing needle

FINISHED SIZE

Length: 39 cm (15½ in) from lobster clasp to end of chain
Crochet piece: 26 x 2 cm (10 x ¾ in)

BEAD SET UP

Thread onto the cotton 108 beads (36 beads for each Bdc row).

NECKBAND

Using 2.00 mm hook, make 73 ch.
Foundation row: 1 dc into 2nd ch from hook, 1 dc into each ch to end, 1 ch turn (72 dc).

Row 1 (WS): 1 Bdc into first dc, 1 dc, * 1 Bdc, 1 dc, rep from * to end, 1 ch turn (36 beads).
Rows 2 and 4 (RS): 1 dc into first dc, 1 dc into each st to end, 1 ch turn.
Row 3: 1 dc into first dc, 1 Bdc, * 1 dc, 1 Bdc, rep from * to end, 1 ch turn.
Row 5: As Row 1.
Cut yarn and fasten off.

FINISHING

Join the lobster clasp to one of the connector findings with the 5 mm jump ring. Thread one of the tail ends onto a sewing needle and sew the connector to the end of the neckband. Join the other connector to the length of chain with the 7 mm jump ring and sew to the other end of the neckband. Neaten ends and trim close.

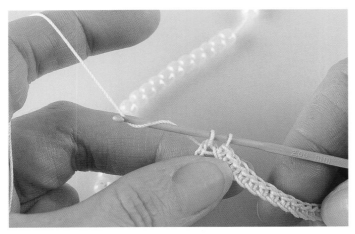

1 *Working 1 double crochet (dc) into each chain to end; preparing to draw through the last two loops on the hook.*

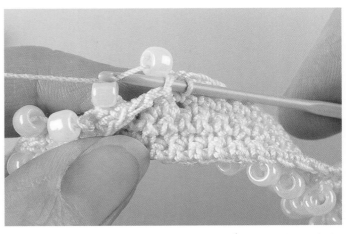

2 *Working a bead double crochet (Bdc) into every other stitch; bringing up a bead and preparing to draw through the first loop.*

3 *Working a double crochet (dc); preparing to draw through the last two loops.*

4 *Sewing the connector holes using the tail ends.*

The wristband

MATERIALS FOR WRISTBAND

- 50 g ball Coats Aida 5 100% crochet cotton (col. 47 Dark Red)
- 40 size 5/0 black opaque seed beads
- 2.00 mm hook
- 15 x 10 mm silver filigree box clasp set
- Sewing needle

FINISHED SIZE

Length (including findings): 18 cm (7 in)

BEAD SET UP

Thread onto the cotton 40 beads (20 beads for each Bdc row).

WRISTBAND

Using 2.00 mm hook, make 41 ch.

Foundation row: 1 dc into 2nd ch from hook, 1 dc into each ch to end, 1 ch turn (40 dc).

Row 1 (WS): 1 Bdc into first dc, 1 dc, * 1 Bdc, 1 dc, rep from * to end, 1 ch turn (20 beads).

Row 2 (RS): 1 dc into first dc, 1 dc into each st to end, 1 ch turn.

Row 3: 1 dc into first dc, 1 Bdc, * 1 dc, 1 Bdc, rep from * to end, 1 ch turn. Cut yarn and fasten off.

FINISHING

Centring one half of the box clasp on the end of the wristband, sew the connector holes with the tail end. Repeat for the other end. Neaten ends and trim close.

The ankleband

MATERIALS FOR ANKLEBAND
- 50 g ball Coats Aida 5 100% crochet cotton (col. 133 Royal Blue)
- 26 size 5/0 silver-lined aqua seed beads
- 2.00 mm hook
- Medium silver lobster clasp
- 8 mm silver jump ring
- Sewing needle

FINISHED SIZE
Length (including findings): 21 cm (8¼ in)

BEAD SET UP
Thread onto the cotton 26 beads.

ANKLEBAND
Using 2.00 mm hook, make 53 ch.

Foundation row: 1 dc into 2nd ch from hook, 1 dc into each ch to end, 1 ch turn (52 dc).

Row 1 (WS): 1 Bdc into first dc, 1 dc, * 1 Bdc, 1 dc, rep from * to end (26 beads).

Cut yarn and fasten off.

FINISHING
Centring the lobster clasp on the end of the ankleband, sew the connector hole with the tail end. Repeat for the other end, sewing the jump ring with the other tail end. Neaten ends and trim close.

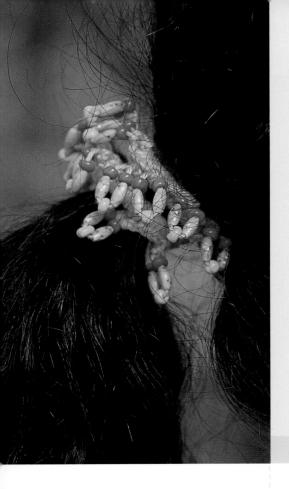

Ponytail bands

Soft cotton yarn is crocheted using the most basic beaded crochet stitches to create fun coverings for plain ponytail bands. The assortment of brightly coloured beads form pretty fringes around the bands. Experiment by making one to suit every outfit.

 **SKILL LEVEL** INTERMEDIATE

- *Captioned step-by-step pictures on page 54.*

SPECIAL INSTRUCTIONS

The dc's are worked round the ponytail band as follows: Insert the hook into the ponytail band, yarn over hook and draw through a loop. Now take the hook over the ponytail band, yarn over hook and draw the yarn through both loops on the hook.

Black bead ponytail band

MATERIALS FOR BLACK PONYTAIL BAND

- Spool of Texere Good Fortune 4 ply cotton (col. Black)
- 19 x 8 mm black glass beads
- 38 size 6/0 opaque turquoise seed beads
- 2.50 mm hook
- Thick 5 cm (2 in) diameter cream ponytail band
- Large-eye darning needle

FINISHED SIZE
Diameter: 8 cm (3¼ in)

BEAD SET UP
Thread onto the cotton *1 turquoise seed, 1 black glass, 1 turquoise seed, rep from * 18 times more. Each repeat represents a 'fringe'.

BLACK PONYTAIL BAND
Using 2.50 mm hook join slip-knot to the ponytail band with a sl.st. Bring up the first fringe to the hook and sl.st to secure, * following the special instructions, work 5 dc, bring up next fringe and sl.st, rep from * until all the beads are worked, ending with 1 dc. Cut yarn and fasten off.

FINISHING
Darn in both tail ends to back of work. Trim close.

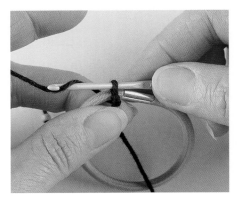

1 *Joining the slip-knot to the ponytail band with a slip stitch (sl.st).*

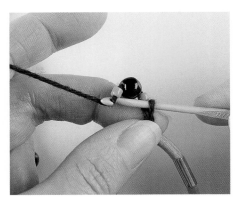

2 *Bringing up the fringe (1 seed, 1 black glass, 1 seed) and working a slip stitch (sl.st).*

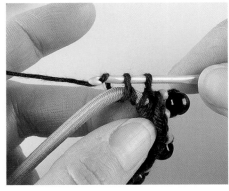

3 *Working a double crochet (dc) around the band; preparing to draw through the last two loops.*

Green fringed ponytail band

MATERIALS FOR GREEN FRINGED PONYTAIL BAND

- Spool of Texere Good Fortune 4 ply cotton (col. Grass)
- 36 size 6/0 opaque orange seed beads
- 18 size 6/0 opaque yellow seed beads
- 36 x 7 mm lime rice beads
- 2.50 mm hook
- Thick 5 cm (2 in) diameter cream ponytail band
- Large-eye darning needle

FINISHED SIZE

Diameter: 9 cm (3½ in)

BEAD SET UP

Thread onto the cotton *1 orange seed, 1 rice bead, 1 yellow seed, 1 rice bead, 1 orange seed, rep from * 17 times more. Each repeat represents a 'fringe'.

GREEN FRINGED PONYTAIL BAND

Using 2.50 mm hook join slip-knot to the ponytail band with a sl.st.
Following the special instructions, work 3 dc, 2 ch, bring up the first fringe to the hook and sl.st to secure, 2 ch, * 5 dc, 2 ch, bring up next fringe, sl.st, 2 ch, rep from * until all the beads are worked, ending with 3 dc.
Cut yarn and fasten off.

FINISHING

Darn in both tail ends to back of work. Trim close.

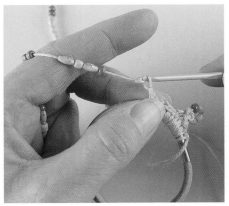

1 *Working a chain stitch (ch).*

2 *Bringing up the fringe and working a slip stitch (sl.st).*

Ball button bracelets

This chunky but elegant modern classic adds a touch of Audrey Hepburn. This bracelet can be made in an evening and is achievable for someone with some crochet experience. Make in one, two or three colours by using the different bead set ups and the same instructions. The double crochet base pulls the beads to form a firm arc shape.

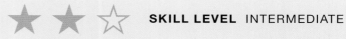

★ ★ ☆   **SKILL LEVEL** INTERMEDIATE

• *Captioned step-by-step pictures on page 56.*

The bracelets

MATERIALS

For one colour:
- Spool of Texere Good Fortune 4 ply cotton (col. Cream)
- 52 x 10 mm cream ball buttons

For two colours:
- Spool of Texere Good Fortune 4 ply cotton (col. Cream)
- 26 x 10 mm cream ball buttons (Main col.)
- 26 x 10 mm dark green ball buttons (Contrast col.)

For three colours:
- Spool of Texere Good Fortune 4 ply cotton (col. Grass)
- 26 x 10 mm cream ball buttons (Main col.)
- 14 x 10 mm lime ball buttons (Contrast col.)
- 12 x 10 mm blue ball buttons (2nd Contrast col.)

- 3.50 mm hook
- 15 x 10 mm silver filigree box clasp set
- Sewing needle

FINISHED SIZE
Length (including findings):
16 cm (6¼ in)

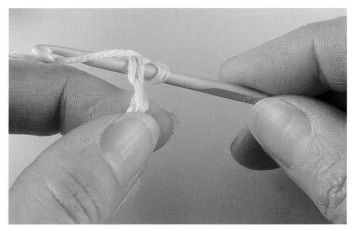

1 *Working 1 double crochet (dc) in the second chain from the hook; preparing to bring the first loop through the chain.*

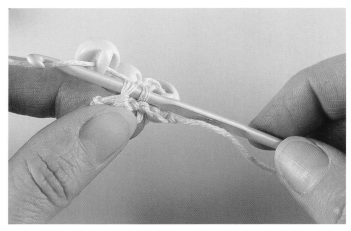

2 *Working a bead double crochet (Bdc) into a stitch; bringing up a bead and preparing to draw through the first loop (the bead sits to the back of the work).*

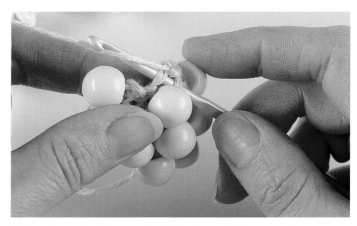

3 *Working a double crochet (dc) into a stitch; preparing to draw through the first loop.*

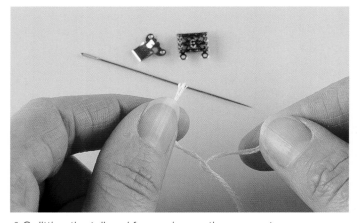

4 *Splitting the tail end for sewing on the connectors.*

5 *Sewing the connectors with the split thread.*

BEAD SET UP (ONE COLOUR)

Thread onto the cotton 52 ball buttons.

BEAD SET UP (TWO COLOURS)

Thread onto the cotton 26 buttons in Main (M) and 26 buttons in Contrast (C) as follows: *1M, 1C, 1M, 2C, 1M, 1C, 1M, rep from * until 52 buttons have been threaded, ending 1C.

BEAD SET UP (THREE COLOURS)

Thread onto the cotton 26 buttons in Main (M), 14 buttons in Contrast (C) and 12 buttons in 2nd Contrast (C2) as follows: 1M, 2C *2M, 2C2, 2M, 2C, rep from * until 52 buttons have been threaded, ending with 1M.

BRACELET

Using 3.50 mm hook, make 5ch.

Row 1 (RS): 1 dc into 2nd ch from hook, 1 dc into each ch to end, 1 ch turn (4 dc).

Row 2 (WS): 1 Bdc into first dc, 1 Bdc into each dc to end (4 beads), 1 ch turn.

Row 3: 1 dc into first st, 1 dc into each st to end, 1 ch turn.

Rep Rows 2 and 3 until all the beads have been crocheted.

Fasten off.

FINISHING

Split the thread of one tail end in two to make a finer thread for sewing. Centring one half of the box clasp on the end of the bracelet, sew the connector holes with the split thread. Repeat for the other end. Neaten ends and trim close.

Curtain ring bracelet and belt

These quick and easy beaded rings are joined to form finished pieces that are inspired by the 1960's. Choose from different size rings and add stunning glass beads for extra sparkle.

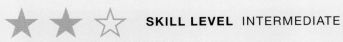

SKILL LEVEL INTERMEDIATE

- *Captioned step-by-step pictures on pages 60–61.*

HOT TIP
Crocheting around a solid form takes a bit of getting used to. Luckily these are small motifs that are quick to work so practise a few to get the tension right before embarking on the real thing.

SPECIAL INSTRUCTIONS

The dc's are worked round the curtain rings as follows: Insert the hook into the curtain ring, yarn over hook and draw through a loop. Now take the hook over the curtain ring, yarn over hook and draw the yarn through both loops on the hook.

The Bdc's are worked round the curtain rings as follows: Insert the hook into the curtain ring, bring up a bead, yarn over hook and draw through a loop bringing the bead to the front of the work. Now take the hook over the curtain ring, yarn over hook and draw the yarn through both loops on the hook.

Joining dc – insert the hook into dc of previous ring worked, yarn over hook and draw through a loop, yarn over hook and draw through both loops on the hook.

The bracelet

MATERIALS FOR BRACELET
- Spool of Texere Good Fortune 4 ply cotton (col. Cerise)
- 80 (approx. 8 g) size 6/0 opaque red seed beads
- 5 x 2.5 cm (1 in) diameter curtain rings
- 2.50 mm hook
- 3 cm (1¼ in) Bali silver shepherd's hook set, including jump rings
- Sewing needle

FINISHED SIZE
Length (including findings): 19 cm (7½ in)

BEAD SET UP
Thread onto the cotton 16 beads for each ring.

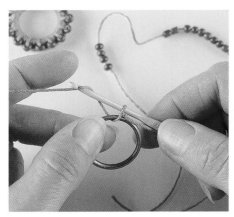

1 *Joining the slip-knot to the ring with a slip stitch (sl.st).*

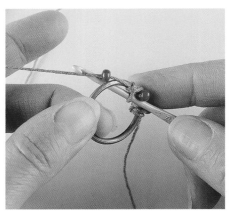

2 *Bdc – Bringing up a bead, yarn over hook and drawing the loop through the ring.*

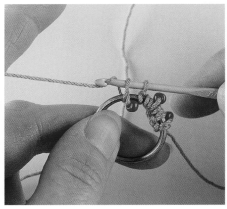

3 *Bdc – Bringing a bead to the front of the work, yarn over hook drawing through 2 loops.*

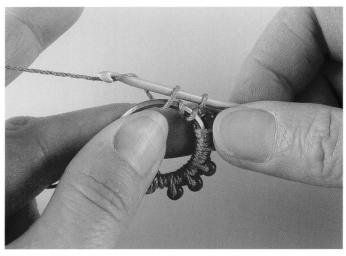

4 *Dc – Taking hook over ring, yarn over hook drawing through 2 loops.*

5 *Joining dc – Inserting the hook into dc of last ring, yarn over hook to draw through a loop. Yoh and finish by drawing through last 2 loops on the hook.*

BRACELET

First ring: Using 2.50 mm hook join the slip-knot to the curtain ring with a sl.st. Following the special instructions, work *1 Bdc, 1 dc, rep from * until all the beads have been worked.
Cut yarn and fasten off.
Subsequent rings (Make 4): Using 2.50 mm hook join the slip-knot to the curtain ring with a sl.st.

Following the special instructions, work *1 Bdc, 1 dc *, rep from * to * until 8 beads have been worked. Now join to the first ring by working a dc between 8th and 9th beads on the first ring. Continue to work from * to * until all the beads have been worked.
Cut yarn and fasten off.

FINISHING

Using the tail ends from an end ring, sew onto the jump ring attached to the shepherd's hook. Repeat for other end. Neaten tail ends and trim close to work.

The belt

MATERIALS FOR BELT

- Spool of Texere Good Fortune 4 ply cotton (col. Turquoise)
- 20 size 6/0 opaque green seed beads (per ring)
- Minimum 17 silver-lined bicoloured (lime/turquoise) 12 mm glass discs
- Minimum 18 x 3 cm (1¼ in) diameter curtain rings
- 2.50 mm hook
- 5.5 cm (2¼ in) gold hook clasp
- Sewing needle

FINISHED SIZE

Length (including findings): 18 rings and 17 glass beads measures 95 cm (37 in)

BEAD SET UP

Thread onto the cotton 20 beads for each ring.

BELT

First ring: Using 2.50 mm hook join the slip-knot to the curtain ring with a sl.st.

Following the special instructions, work *1 Bdc, 1 dc, rep from * until all the beads have been worked.
Leaving a 7 cm (2¾ in) tail end, cut yarn and fasten off.
Cut yarn and fasten off.
Repeat until required number of crocheted rings has been completed.

FINISHING

Thread one of the tail ends through a glass bead and join to the double crochet between beads ten and eleven of previous ring. Thread back through the glass bead and neaten off both tail ends. Continue to join all the rings until desired length. Sew the hook clasps between beads ten and eleven of each end ring. Neaten off.

1 *Threading a tail through a glass bead and into the double crochet (dc) between beads 10 and 11 of the previous ring.*

2 *Threading back through the glass bead ready for neatening off.*

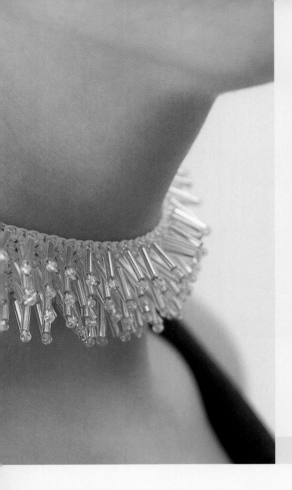

White fringed choker

A modern take on the 'Punk Rock' dog collar, this elegant choker, crocheted in fine mercerised cotton, is soft to the touch and comfortable to wear. Although crocheted throughout in simple double crochet, it has been given an Intermediate skill level due to the number of beads involved. Follow the Hot tip to speed up the make process.

★ ★ ☆   **SKILL LEVEL** INTERMEDIATE

- *Captioned step-by-step pictures on pages 64–65.*

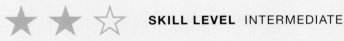

HOT TIP

Thread enough beads to work a single fringed row. The yarn will be broken after each following double crochet row allowing the set of beads to be threaded for the next fringed row. Although this will mean breaking the yarn at the end of every other row, it will save the frustration of pulling enough yarn through the beads to complete each double crochet row. Despite the extra darning in, the overall make will be faster.

FINISHED SIZE

Length (including findings): 39 cm (15½ in)

Length of crochet: 25 cm (10 in) The length of the choker can be adjusted with the use of the chained clasp set.

BEAD SET UP

For each fringe, thread onto the cotton *1 seed, 1 bugle, 1 seed, 1 bugle, 1 seed, rep from * until 45 fringes are threaded for Foundation row. When the Foundation row has been worked, thread up the same number of fringes for Row 2 and repeat this process for Rows 4 and 6.

The choker

MATERIALS

- 100 g Coats Eldorado mercerised cotton (col. 4250 White)
- 361 (approx. 30 g) 10 mm silver bugle beads
- 542 (approx. 14 g) size 9/0 crystal seed beads
- 2.00 mm hook

- Medium silver lobster clasp
- 5 mm silver jump ring
- 7 mm silver jump ring
- 2 silver end connectors (5 holes on 1 side and 1 on the other)
- 8 cm (3¼ in) length of silver chain
- 25 mm silver head pin
- Sewing needle
- Round-nose pliers

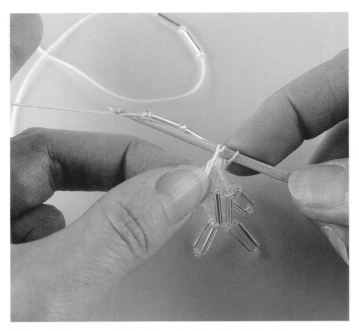

1 *Foundation row: Frdc – Inserting the hook into the next chain (ch) and bringing up the beads for 1 fringe, yarn over hook to draw through a loop. Finish as for Step 4.*

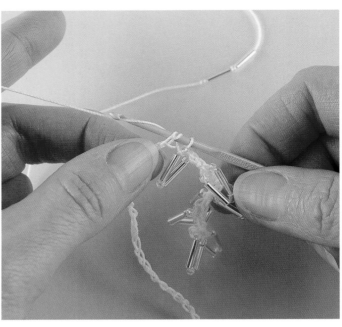

2 *Foundation row: Dc – Inserting the hook into the next chain (ch), yarn over hook to draw through a loop. Finish as for Step 4.*

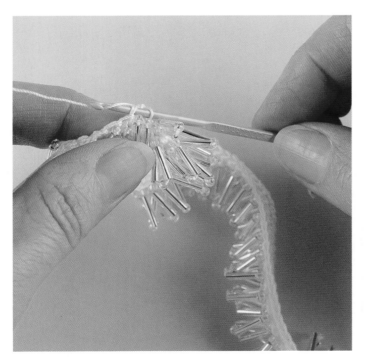

3 *Row 1: Dc – Inserting the hook into the next double crochet (dc), yarn over hook to draw through a loop. Finish as for Step 4.*

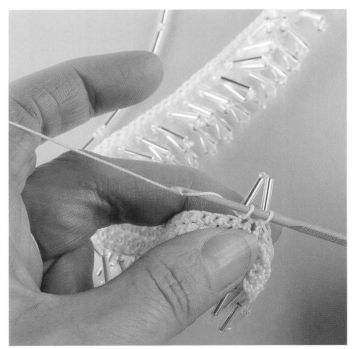

4 *To complete a dc and Frdc – Yarn over hook to draw through the last 2 loops (fringe sits to back of work for Frdc).*

CHOKER

Using 2.00 mm hook, make 91 ch.

Foundation row: 1 Frdc into second ch from hook, 1 dc into next ch, * 1 Frdc into next ch, 1 dc into next ch, rep from * to end, 1 ch turn.

Row 1 (RS): 1 dc into first dc, 1 dc into each st to end. Break yarn, thread on 45 fringes, rejoin yarn, 1 ch turn.

Row 2 (WS): *1 dc into first dc, 1 Frdc into next dc, rep from * to end, 1 ch turn.

Rows 3 and 5: As Row 1.

Row 4: *1 Frdc into first dc, 1 dc into next dc, rep from * to end.

Row 6: As Row 2.

Cut yarn and fasten off.

FINISHING

Join the lobster clasp to one of the connector findings with the 5 mm jump ring. Thread one of the tail ends onto the sewing needle and sew the connector to the end of the choker. Join the other connector to the length of chain with the 7 mm jump ring and sew to the other end of the choker. Neaten ends and trim close to work. Thread a seed bead, a bugle bead and a seed bead onto the head pin. Using round-nose pliers, bend the top of the pin over and thread through the last link in the chain. Close loop to secure.

5 *Joining in – Inserting hook into first dc drawing through a loop of fresh yarn. Leaving a 3 cm (1¼ in) tail end, work 1 chain (ch) to start the new row.*

6 *Sewing the connector holes using the tail ends.*

Purple disc bracelet and earring set

The combination of purple, lime green and the lightest blue gives this set a very 1970's feel. The discs and seed beads crocheted in pairs create the movement and volume to make these pieces really sparkle. Make the bracelet and earring set, then treat yourself to a new outfit and go out and party!

★ ☆ ☆ **SKILL LEVEL** EASY

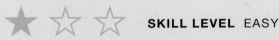
• *Captioned step-by-step pictures on page 68.*

HOT TIP

Make sure that the discs have the hole at the top, rather than centrally, as found in sequins: this will allow the discs to hang rather than be fixed flat. Shake the pieces on completion to separate the discs and give more movement.

SPECIAL INSTRUCTIONS

The bicone beads are crocheted singularly whilst the seed beads and discs are crocheted in pairs throughout. Whilst the seed beads are crocheted over the seed beads of the previous row, the discs are crocheted over the bicones and vice versa.

The bracelet

MATERIALS FOR BRACELET

- Small spool of 0.20 mm (36 swg) black wire
- 68 x 15 mm diameter purple discs
- 34 x 6 mm clear finish bicone lime glass beads
- 128 size 10/0 silver-lined light aqua seed beads
- 2.50 mm hook
- 3 cm (1¼ in) Bali silver shepherd's hook set, including jump rings
- Sewing needle

FINISHED SIZE

Length (including findings): 20 cm (8 in)

BEAD SET UP

Thread onto wire [*2 discs, 2 seeds, 1 bicone, 2 seeds*, rep from * to * 7 times more, 2 discs, 1 bicone **2 seeds, 2 discs, 2 seeds, 1 bicone**, rep from ** to ** 7 times more] twice.

BRACELET

Using 2.50 mm hook

Foundation row: Work 1 ch, 33 Bch. N.B. the last Bch will be worked with a bicone, 1 ch turn.

Row 1: Following the special instructions, work 1 Bdc into first and every st to the end. N.B. the row will begin and end with 2 discs, 1 ch turn.

Row 2: As Row 1, but the row will begin and end with bicones, 1 ch turn.

Row 3: As Row 1.

Cut wire and fasten off.

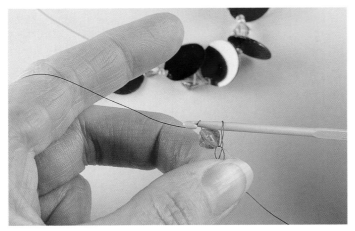

1 *Working a bead chain (Bch) using a glass bicone.*

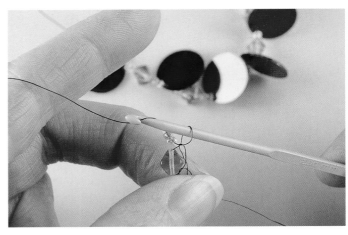

2 *Working a bead chain (Bch) using two seed beads.*

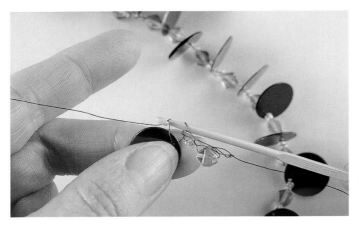

3 *Working a bead chain (Bch) using two discs.*

4 *Working a bead double crochet (Bdc) using two discs over a bicone of the previous row.*

5 *Working a bead double crochet (Bdc) using a bicone over the discs of the previous row.*

6 *Using the tail end to sew on a finding.*

FINISHING

Using the tail end from one end, sew on the jump ring attached to the shepherd's hook. Repeat for other end. Neaten tails ends and trim close to work.

The earrings

MATERIALS FOR EARRINGS

- Small spool of 0.20 mm (36 swg) black wire
- 40 x 15 mm diameter purple discs
- 22 x 6 mm clear finish bicone lime glass beads
- 72 size 10/0 silver-lined light aqua seed beads
- 2.50 mm hook
- 2 silver fishhook earring wires
- Sewing needle

FINISHED SIZE

Length: 9 cm (3½ in) to bend of fishhook

BEAD SET UP

Thread onto wire *1 bicone, 2 seeds, 2 discs, 2 seeds*, rep from * to * twice more, 1 bicone, 2 discs, **2 seeds, 1 bicone, 2 seeds, 2 discs**, rep from ** to ** twice more and from * to * 3 times, 1 bicone.

EARRING

Using 2.50 mm hook.
Foundation row: Work 13 Bch.
N.B: the last Bch will be worked with a bicone, 1 ch turn.
Row 1: Following the special instructions, work 1 Bdc into first and every st to the end. N.B the last Bdc will be worked with 2 discs, 1 ch turn.
Row 2: As Row 1 with the last Bdc being worked with the last bicone. Cut wire and fasten off.

FINISHING

Thread up one of the tail wires and use to sew the fishhook earring wire. Neaten off both tail ends and trim close to work. Holding the earring wire, shake the earring gently to allow the discs to fall in a down-wards position.

Silver sequin and crystal bracelet

The quirky texture of the long bugle beads, the tiny cuts of crystal-style glass and the silver sequins combine to create a piece that wouldn't look out of place at the best Ice Hotel reception. For a really special occasion, the silver plate wire can be replaced with solid silver wire of the same thickness.

★ ★ ☆ **SKILL LEVEL** INTERMEDIATE

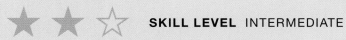

• *Captioned step-by-step pictures on pages 72–73.*

HOT TIP
Practise on a small sample to get used to the strange shapes – the bugle beads will deliberately sit at an angle. The beauty of this pattern is that the sequins and bugle beads lie above those of the previous wrong side row allowing the stitches to be easily lined up.

SPECIAL INSTRUCTIONS

The sequins and bugle beads are worked on the wrong side rows with the seed beads added on the right side rows. The bugle beads and sequins are worked individually throughout.

On the right side rows, the seed beads are worked together in pairs and on the wrong side rows they are again worked in pairs, sandwiching each sequin.

The bracelet

MATERIALS
- Small spool of 0.20 mm (36 swg) silver-plated wire
- 64 x 10 mm silver sequins
- 398 (approx. 8 g) size 9/0 crystal seed beads
- 48 (approx. 3 g) 10 mm silver bugle beads
- 2.00 mm hook
- Two 15 x 10 mm silver filigree box clasp sets
- Sewing needle

FINISHED SIZE
Length (including findings): 16.5 cm (6½ in)

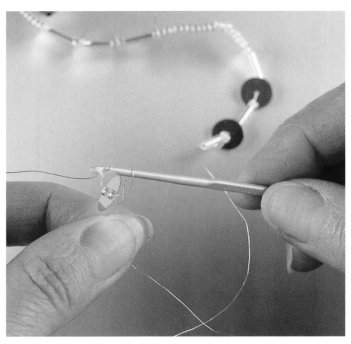

1 *Working a bead chain (Bch) using a seed bead, a sequin and a seed bead.*

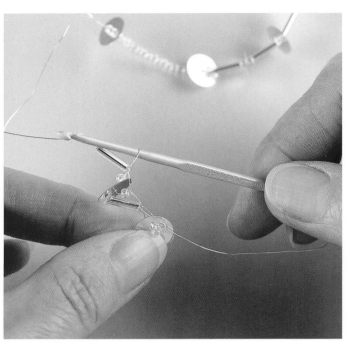

2 *Working a bead chain (Bch) using a bugle bead.*

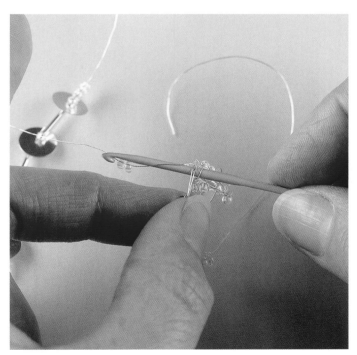

3 *Working a bead double crochet (Bdc) using two seed beads; preparing to draw through the first loop. Yoh and finish by drawing through the last two loops on the hook.*

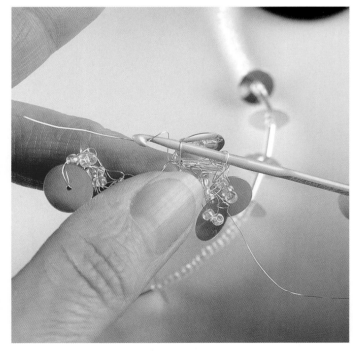

4 *Working a bead double crochet (Bdc) using a seed bead, a sequin and a seed bead; preparing to draw through the last two loops on the hook.*

BEAD SET UP

Thread onto the wire *1 seed, 1 sequin, 1 seed, [1 bugle, 1 seed, 1 sequin, 1 seed] twice more, 18 seed, rep from * until 15 repeats have been threaded, 1 seed, 1 sequin, 1 seed, [1 bugle, 1 seed, 1 sequin, 1 seed] twice more.

BRACELET

Using 2.00 mm hook and following the special instructions, work 7 Bch, 1 Bch turn.

Foundation row (RS): 1 Bdc into 2nd Bch from hook and into every Bch to end, N.B. 7 seed beads Bdc worked, 1 Bch turn.

Row 1 (WS): 1 Bdc into first st and into every st to end, N.B. 4 sequin Bdc and 3 bugle bead Bdc worked, 1 Bch turn.

Row 2: 1 Bdc into first st and into every st to end, N.B. 7 seed beads Bdc worked, 1 Bch turn.

Rep Rows 1 and 2 until 30 rows in total have been completed.

Cut wire and fasten off.

FINISHING

Placing one half of the box clasps at each corner of one end of the bracelet, sew the connector holes with the wire tails. Repeat for the other end. Neaten ends and trim close.

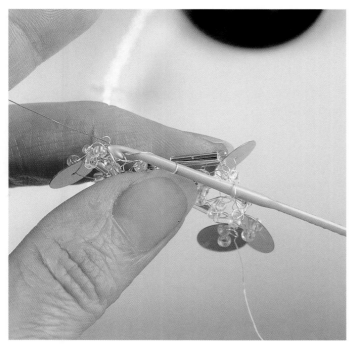

5 *Working a bead double crochet (Bdc) using a bugle bead; preparing to draw through the last two loops on the hook. The bugle bead sits at an angle at the back of the work.*

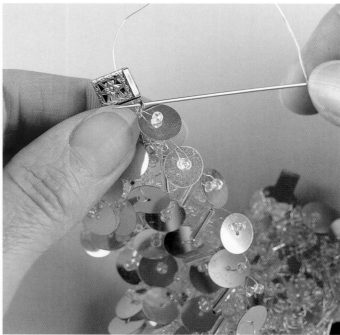

6 *Using the tail end to sew on a finding.*

Gold and iris sequin necklace and ring set

A layering of square sequins gives real depth to this necklace. Gold sequins are sandwiched between Aurora Boralis or iris sequins and interspersed with tiny silver-lined seed beads to create sparkle. Each pendant is individually made and the three pieces are joined with a simple bead chain stitch.

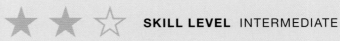

SKILL LEVEL INTERMEDIATE

• *Captioned step-by-step pictures on page 76.*

SPECIAL INSTRUCTIONS

Bch – Bead chain with seed beads crocheted in pairs

Bdc – Bead double crochet with seed beads crocheted in pairs

B5dc – Bead double crochet, bringing up a seed bead, an iris sequin, a gold sequin, an iris sequin and a seed bead in the same stitch

The necklace

MATERIALS FOR NECKLACE

- Small spool of 0.20 mm (36 swg) gunbronze wire
- 48 x 7 mm iris sequins
- 24 x 7 mm gold sequins
- Tube of silver-lined candy mix size 10/0 seed beads
- 2.00 mm hook
- Small gold lobster clasp
- 7 mm gold jump ring
- 2 x 5 mm gold jump rings
- Sewing needle

FINISHED SIZE

Length (including findings): 43 cm (17 in)
Each sequin pendant is 3.5 cm (1½ in) long by 1.5 cm (⅝ in) wide.

BEAD SET UP

Each pendant

Thread onto the wire 3 seed, ** [1 Iris sequin, 1 gold sequin, 1 iris sequin, 4 seed] 3 times, 1 iris, 1 gold, 1 iris ** 24 seed, rep from ** to ** once, 19 seed.

NECKLACE

Sequined pendants (make three)
Using 2.00 mm hook and following the special instructions, make 9 Bch.
Foundation row (WS): 1 B5dc into second Bch from hook, 1 Bdc into next Bch, *1 B5dc into next Bch, 1 Bdc into next Bch, rep from * to end, 1 Bch turn.
Row 1 (RS): 1 Bdc into first st, 1 Bdc into each st to end, 1 Bch turn.
Row 2: * 1 B5dc, 1 Bdc, rep from * to end.
Cut wire and fasten off.

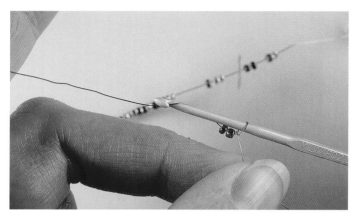

1 *Pendant and ring: Working a bead chain (Bch) using two seed beads; preparing to draw through to form the first Bch.*

2 *Pendant and ring: Working a bead double crochet (Bdc) using two seed beads.*

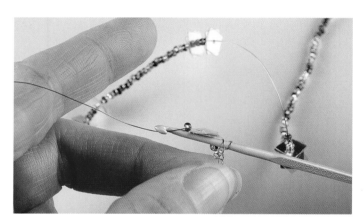

3 *Pendant and ring: B5dc – Working a bead double crochet (Bdc) using a seed bead, an iris sequin, a gold sequin, an iris sequin and a seed bead in the same stitch.*

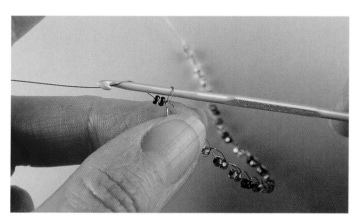

4 *Beaded chain: Working a bead chain (Bch) using two seed beads; preparing to draw through to form a Bch.*

5 *Beaded chain: Working the bead double crochet (Bdc), using two seed beads, across the end of a sequinned pendant.*

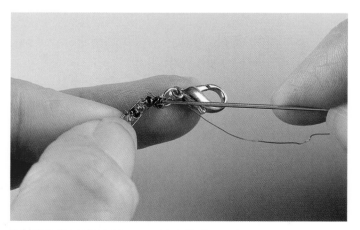

6 *Using the tail end to sew on a finding.*

BEADED CHAIN BEAD SET UP

Thread onto the wire 170 seed beads.

BEADED CHAIN

Using 2.00 mm hook and following the special instructions, make 35 Bch, * work 3 Bdc across one end of the first sequinned pendant, 3 Bch, rep from * twice more, work 32 Bch to finish.

FINISHING

Attach a 5 mm jump ring to the lobster clasp and close to secure. Join the jump ring to the necklace by threading the tail end through the jump ring and the first beads four times until secure. Finish by threading the tail wire through the first four beads and trim the wire close to the work. Repeat for the other end, attaching the 5 mm jump ring to the 7 mm jump ring to create a fastening for the lobster clasp.

Trim ends close to work.

The ring

MATERIALS FOR RING

- Small spool of 0.20 mm (36 swg) gunbronze wire
- 32 x 7 mm iris sequins
- 16 x 7 mm gold sequins
- Tube of silver-lined candy mix size 10/0 seed beads
- 2.00 mm hook
- Sewing needle

FINISHED SIZE

7 cm (2¾ in) long by 1.5 cm (⅝ in) wide

BEAD SET UP

Thread onto the wire 3 seed **[1 iris sequin, 1 gold sequin, 1 iris sequin, 4 seed] 7 times, 1 iris, 1 gold, 1 iris**, 40 seed, rep from ** to ** ending with 35 seed.

RING

Using 2.00 mm hook and following the special instructions, make 17 Bch.

Foundation row (WS): 1 B5dc into second Bch from hook, 1 Bdc into next Bch, *1 B5dc into next Bch, 1 Bdc into next Bch, rep from * to end, 1 Bch turn.

Row 1 (RS): 1 Bdc into first stitch, 1 Bdc into each stitch to end, 1 Bch turn.

Row 2: *1 B5dc, 1 Bdc, rep from * to end.

Cut wire and fasten off.

FINISHING

Bend piece to form a circle. Thread one of the tail ends onto a needle and slipstitch to form a flat seam. Neaten off both tail ends through the seed beads. Trim close to work.

Beaded mesh choker

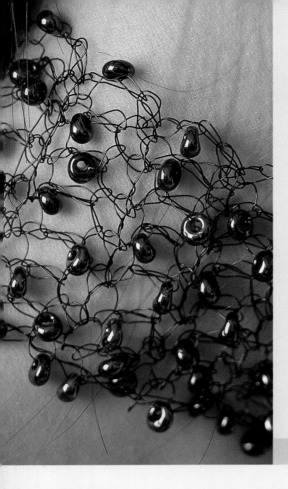

The effect of a fine black mesh with a scattering of dark iridescent seed beads produces an extremely flattering choker. Once the technique of introducing the beads to the two stages of the treble stitch is mastered, the piece can be produced very quickly. The beauty of working this project is that the odd mistake doesn't really show – perfect!

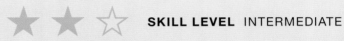

SKILL LEVEL INTERMEDIATE

• *Captioned step-by-step pictures on pages 80–81.*

HOT TIP
If you feel confident enough, the piece could be lengthened to produce a wonderful belt to team with a pair of denims, alternatively make a piece measuring approximately 14 cm (5½ in) to make a bracelet.

SPECIAL INSTRUCTIONS

Btr – Bead treble Yarn over hook and insert hook into next stitch, yarn over hook, draw loop through work, bring a bead next to the loop on the hook, yarn over hook and draw through two loops, yarn over hook and draw through the remaining two loops.

Btr2 – Bead treble with bead introduced before second 'yoh draw through two loops' Yarn over hook and insert hook into next stitch, yarn over hook, draw loop through work, yarn over hook and draw through two loops, bring a bead next to the loop on the hook, yarn over hook and draw through the remaining two loops.

The choker

MATERIALS
• Small spool of 0.20 mm (36 swg) black wire
• 176 (approx. 8 g) size 7/0 iridescent rainbow seed beads
• 2.50 mm hook
• Medium gold lobster clasp
• 5 mm gold jump ring
• 7 mm gold jump ring
• 2 gold end connectors (3 holes on 1 side and 1 hole on the other)
• 8 cm (3¼ in) length of gold chain
• Sewing needle

FINISHED SIZE
Length: 40 cm (15¾ in) from lobster clasp to end of chain

1 *Using the wire end, threading on a minimum of 200 beads.*

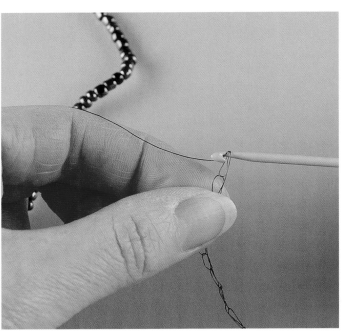

2 *Working 10 chain stitches (ch).*

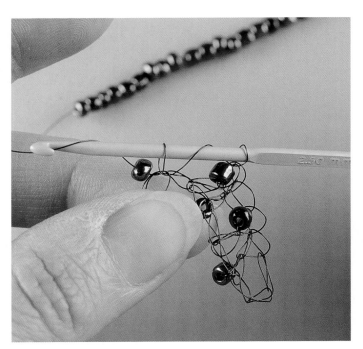

3 *Btr – Bringing up a bead next to the loop on the hook, yarn over hook and draw through two loops. Yarn over hook and finish by drawing through the last two loops on the hook.*

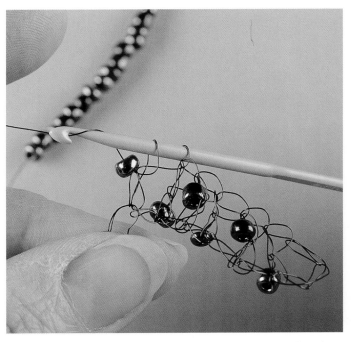

4 *Btr2 – Bringing up a bead before the last stage of a bead treble crochet (Btr), yarn over hook to draw through the remaining two loops.*

Length of crochet: 28 x 4 cm (11 x 1½ in). The length of the choker can be adjusted with the use of the chained clasp set.

BEAD SET UP

Thread onto the wire a minimum of 200 beads, approx. 43 cm (17 in).

CHOKER

Using 2.50 mm hook, make 10 ch.

Foundation row: 1 Btr2 into 4th chain from hook, *1 Btr, 1 Btr2, rep from * to end, 1 Bch turn.

Row 1 (RS): 1 dc into first st, 1 dc into each st to end, 1 ch, 1 Bch, 1 ch turn.

Row 2: 1 Btr2 into 2nd stitch, *1 Btr , 1 Btr2, rep from * to end, 1 Bch turn.

Rep Rows 1 and 2 until work measures 28 cm (11 in).

Cut wire and fasten off.

FINISHING

Join the lobster clasp to one of the connector findings with the 5 mm jump ring. Thread one of the tail ends onto a sewing needle and sew the connector to the end of the choker. Join the other connector to the length of chain with the 7 mm jump ring and sew to the other end of the choker. Neaten ends and trim close to work.

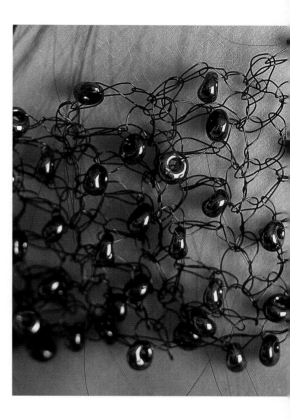

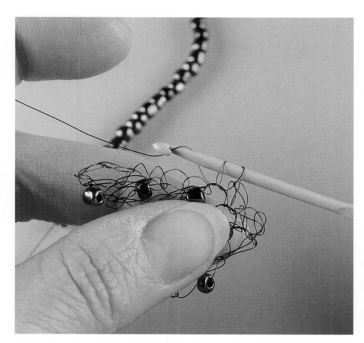

5 *Working a double crochet (dc) into each stitch to the end of the row; preparing to draw through the last two loops on the hook.*

6 *Using the tail end to sew on a finding.*

Black jet chevron choker

The combination of the popular chevron crochet stitch pattern and black jet beads creates a modern interpretation of early 20th century 'mourning' jewellery. The faceted black jet beads used are plastic, making the choker light and comfortable to wear.

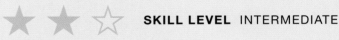

SKILL LEVEL INTERMEDIATE

• *Captioned step-by-step pictures on pages 84–85.*

HOT TIP

Use small safety pins as markers for each point, i.e. to mark the centre treble of each shell stitch and to mark the stitch created from the clusters.

SPECIAL INSTRUCTIONS

Btr – Bead treble Wrap the yarn over the hook and insert the hook into the next stitch (or the fourth chain from hook for the Foundation row). Wrap the yarn over the hook and draw the yarn through the work to form a third loop on the hook. Slide a bead next to the loop on the hook, yarn over the hook and draw the yarn through the first two loops on the hook; wrap again, drawing through the remaining two loops on the hook.

Sh – Shell Work three treble into next stitch.

Bsh – Bead shell As above, but working second treble as Btr.

Tr3tog – Treble cluster over three stitches * Wrap the yarn over the hook and insert the hook into the next stitch, wrap the yarn over the hook and draw the yarn through the work to form another loop on the hook, yarn over hook, draw through two loops, rep from * twice more (four loops on hook), yarn over hook, draw through all loops.

Tr2tog – Treble cluster over two stitches As Tr3tog but work from * twice (three loops on hook), yarn over hook, draw through all loops.

Btr3tog – Bead treble cluster over three stitches * Yarn over, insert hook into next stitch, yarn over hook, draw loop through work, yarn over hook, draw through two loops *, rep from * to * twice more, placing a bead before last repeat. Yarn over hook draw through four loops on hook.

Btr2tog – Bead treble cluster over two stitches As Btr3tog, but work from * to * twice, placing a bead after second repeat, draw through three loops on hook.

1 *Btr – Bringing up a bead next to the loop on the hook, preparing to draw through two loops. Yoh and finish by drawing through last two loops on the hook.*

The Choker

MATERIALS

- Small spool of 0.20 mm (36 swg) black wire
- Forty-two 12 x 6 mm plastic faceted black opaque pendants
- 6 size 9/0 black seed beads
- 2.00 mm hook
- Medium silver lobster clasp
- 5 mm silver jump ring
- 7 mm silver jump ring
- 2 silver end connectors (5 holes on one side and 1 hole on the other)
- 8 cm (3¼ in) length of silver chain
- 25 mm silver head pin
- Sewing needle
- Round-nose pliers

FINISHED SIZE

Length: 40 cm (15¾ in) from lobster clasp to end of chain

BEAD SET UP

Thread onto the wire 42 black opaque pendant beads.

CHOKER

Using 2.00 mm hook, make 72 chs.

Foundation row (WS): 1 Btr into 3rd ch from hook, * 1 tr into each of next 2 ch, 1 Btr into next ch, 1 tr into each of next 2 ch, 1 Bsh into next ch, 1 tr into each of next 2 ch, 1 Btr into next ch, 1 tr into next 2 ch, work a Btr3tog over next 3 ch, work from * 4 times more, ending with Btr2tog over last 2 ch, 2 ch turn.

Row 1: 1 tr into each of next 6 tr, * 1 sh into next tr, 1 tr into each of next 5 tr, tr3tog over next 3 sts, 1 tr into each of next 5 tr, rep from * 3 times more, 1 sh into next tr, 1 tr into each of next 5 tr, tr2tog over last 2 sts, 2 ch turn.

Row 2: 1 Btr into next tr, * 1 tr into each of next 2 tr, 1 Btr into next tr, 1 tr into

each of next 2 tr, 1 Bsh into next tr, 1 tr into each of next 2 tr, 1 Btr into next tr, 1 tr into each of next 2 tr, Btr3tog over next 3 sts, rep from * 4 times more, ending with Btr2tog over last 2 trs. Cut wire and fasten off.

FINISHING

Join the lobster clasp to one of the connector findings with the 5 mm jump ring. Thread one of the tail ends onto a sewing needle and sew the connector to the end of the choker. Join the other connector to the length of chain with the 7 mm jump ring and sew to the other end of the choker. Neaten ends and trim close to work. Thread the seed beads onto the head pin. Using round-nose pliers, bend the top of the pin over and thread through the last link in the chain. Close loop to secure.

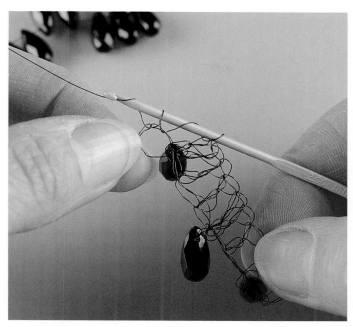

2 *Bsh – Working third treble into the same stitch to form a shell. The second treble worked as a bead treble crochet (Btr), see Step 1.*

3 *Btr3tog – Preparing to draw through the last four loops on the hook, having placed a bead before the third repeat.*

4 *Btr2tog – Preparing to draw through the last three loops on the hook, having placed a bead after the second repeat.*

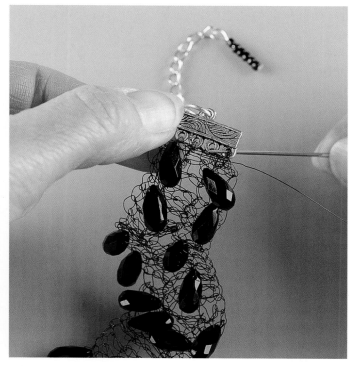

5 *Using the tail end to sew on a finding.*

Glass beads and purple pearls ring

Unusual purple pearls are used as a pretty backdrop to the iridescent glass beads. The glass beads are secured with large chain stitches that are gently pulled to shape when finishing. The fine wire produces a comfortable ring that moulds to the finger to produce a piece that is the height of fashion.

★ ★ ☆ **SKILL LEVEL** INTERMEDIATE

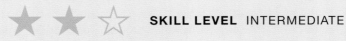

• Captioned step-by-step pictures on page 88.

HOT TIP

To make the ring larger, add 6 pearls at the beginning and the end of bead set up, working the extra beads into double crochet rows before and after the glass bead rows.

Row 5: 1 Bdc into first dc, make a Bch extending chain loop to the length of a glass bead, 1 Bdc into last dc, 1 ch turn. Repeat Row 5 three times more.
Row 9: 1 Bdc into first dc, make 4 ch, 1 Bdc into last dc, 1 ch turn.
Rows 10–14: As Row 1.
Cut wire and fasten off.

FINISHING

Gently stretch the piece lengthways to allow the glass beads to lie flat within the work. Thread one of the tail ends onto a needle and slip stitch ends to form a flat seam. Neaten off both tail ends into the work. Trim close to work.

The ring

MATERIALS

- Small spool of 0.20 mm (36 swg) gunbronze wire
- 70 x 3 mm purple pearls
- Four 10 x 8 mm Indian iridescent teal glass twisted tubes
- 2.00 mm hook
- Sewing needle

FINISHED SIZE

7 cm (2 ¾ in) long x 2 cm (¾ in) wide

BEAD SET UP

Thread onto the wire 33 pearls, 1 glass bead, *2 pearls, 1 glass bead, rep from * twice more, 31 pearls.

RING

Using 2.00 mm hook, work 7 ch.
Foundation row: 1 Bdc into 2nd chain from hook, 1 Bdc into each ch to end, 1 ch turn (6 Bdc).
Row 1: 1 Bdc into first dc, 1 Bdc into each st to end, 1 ch turn.
Rep Row 1 three times more.

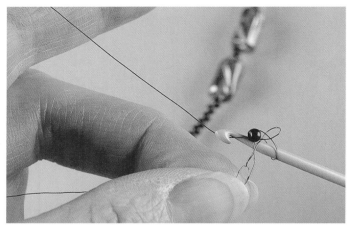

1 *Working 1 bead double crochet (Bdc) in second chain from the hook.*

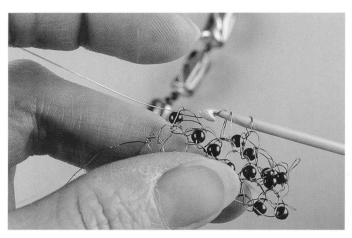

2 *Bdc – Preparing to draw through the last two loops on the hook.*

3 *Bch – extending the chain loop to the length of the glass bead.*

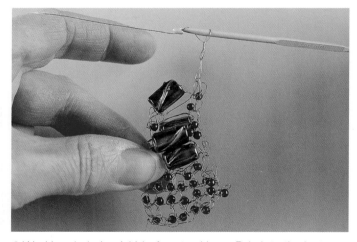

4 *Working 4 chains (ch) before working a Bdc into the last stitch after the glass bead.*

5 *Using the tail end to slip stitch (sl.st) the seam.*

Spiral crochet bracelet

Seed beads that are tonally close are worked in alternate double crochet stitches to form a heavyweight spiralled piece that just oozes sophistication. The bracelet is topped off with two statement glass beads and a chunky bar and toggle set.

 **SKILL LEVEL** ADVANCED

• *Captioned step-by-step pictures on page 90.*

HOT TIP

Rope crochet is tricky to get started, but once a couple of spirals have been formed it takes shape quite quickly. After a couple of spirals, form a tube by gently opening up the inside of the work using the end of a thicker crochet hook. Leave a 15 cm (6 in) tail at the beginning and end of the piece for joining the accent beads and the findings.

SPECIAL INSTRUCTIONS

In order to form the beads on the outside of the tube, the piece is worked from the inside. Each Bdc is worked into the back loop of the stitch below.

The bracelet

MATERIALS
• 50 g ball Coats Aida 5 100% crochet cotton (col. 133 Royal Blue)
• 175 (approx. 16 g) size 7/0 silver-lined bronze seed beads
• 175 (approx. 16 g) size 7/0 silver-lined royal blue seed beads
• Two 18 x 14 mm silver-lined bicoloured (purple/lime) twisted lozenges
• 2.00 mm hook
• 22 x 20 mm (1 x ¾ in) pewter bar and toggle ring set
• Sewing needle

FINISHED SIZE
Length (including end beads and findings): 22 cm (8¾ in)

BEAD SET UP
Thread onto the cotton *1 blue, 1 bronze, rep from * until all beads have been threaded.

BRACELET
Using 2.00 mm hook, work 5 ch and join with a sl.st to form a ring.
Work 7 Bdc into ring, DO NOT JOIN.
Following the special instructions, continue to work in a spiral until work measures 16 cm (6¼ in).
Cut yarn and fasten off.

FINISHING

Using a sewing needle, thread one tail end through the glass bead, the connector hole on the toggle ring and back through the glass bead. Take up a stitch from the crochet end and repeat twice more until the bead and finding are securely attached. Repeat for the other end, joining the connector hole on the toggle bar (making sure that enough slack is given to allow the bar to pass through the ring). Neaten off ends and trim close.

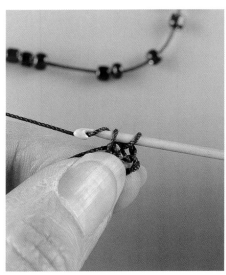

1 *Working bead doube crochet (Bdc) into the 5 ch ring; preparing to draw through the last two loops of a Bdc.*

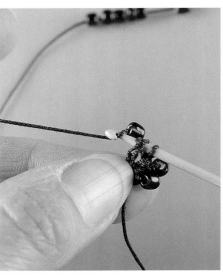

2 *Getting started in the spiral; bringing up a bead and working into the back loop of the stitch below.*

3 *Working in a spiral. The piece is crocheted from the inside working in an anti-clockwise direction.*

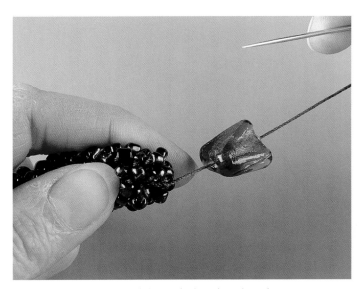

4 *Threading the tail end through the glass bead.*

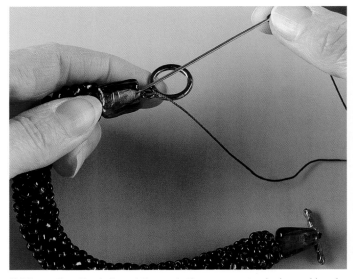

5 *Threading the tail end through the connector hole and back through the glass bead, taking up a stitch from the crocheted end until the findings are secure.*

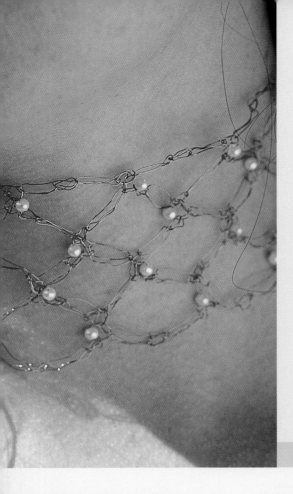

Solomon knot chokers

The Solomon's knot stitch takes a bit of practice, but once mastered it is very quick to work. The result is a beautifully delicate wide choker that moulds softly to the neck. The adjustable clasp findings allow the choker to fit all sizes. The choker has been worked in two colours; try gold and green sparkle for the evening or pale bronze with tiny pearls for a wedding.

★ ★ ★ **SKILL LEVEL** ADVANCED

• *Captioned step-by-step pictures on pages 94–95.*

HOT TIP

Practise getting the stitch lengths right before embarking on the main piece. It is important that the piece doesn't end up too baggy, as it needs some body to fit tight to the neck.

SPECIAL INSTRUCTIONS

Solomon Knot stitch Make a chain and lengthen the loop. Yarn over hook, keeping the single back thread separate from the front two threads with your thumb, draw loop through. Work a double crochet into this single back thread to complete one Solomon's knot stitch. The stitch is worked in two lengths as detailed here.

ESK – Edge Solomon's Knot These form the foundation chains and edges of the piece. The total length of this stitch should be 1 cm (⅜ in).

BESK – Bead Edge Solomon's Knot As above, adding a bead to the double crochet.

MSK – Main Solomon's Knot This stitch forms the main body of the piece. The stitches are roughly one third longer than the ESK's, making the total length of the stitch 1.5 cm (⅝ in).

The chokers

MATERIALS FOR GOLD FILIGREE CHOKER WITH GREEN GLASS BEADS

- Small spool of 0.20 mm (36 swg) light gold wire
- 47 size 8/0 iridescent green seed beads
- 2.00 mm hook
- Medium gold lobster clasp
- 5 mm gold jump ring
- 7 mm gold jump ring
- 2 gold end connectors (3 holes on one side and 1 hole on the other)
- 8 cm (3¼ in) length of gold chain
- Sewing needle

MATERIALS FOR GUNBRONZE FILIGREE CHOKER WITH WHITE PEARLS

- Small spool of 0.20 mm (36 swg) gunbronze wire
- 47 x 3 mm white pearls
- 2.00 mm hook
- Medium gold lobster clasp
- 5 mm gold jump ring
- 7 mm gold jump ring
- 2 gold end connectors (3 holes on one side and 1 hole on the other)
- 8 cm (3¼ in) length of gold chain
- Sewing needle

FINISHED SIZE

Length of crochet piece: 28 cm (11 in). The length can be adjusted with the use of the chained clasp set.

BEAD SET UP

Thread onto the wire 47 beads or pearls.

CHOKER

Foundation row: Using 2.00 mm hook, work 2 ch, 1 dc into 2nd ch from hook, make 22 ESK's ending with 1 MSK, turn.

Row 1: 1 Bdc into dc between 3rd and 4th loops from hook * 2 MSK, miss 2 loops, 1 Bdc into next dc, rep from * to end, turn.

Row 2: Work 1 BESK, 1 ESK and 1 MSK, 1 Bdc into dc between 4th and 5th loops from hook * 2 MSK, miss 2 loops, 1 Bdc into next dc, rep from * ending in top of ESK, turn. Rep Row 2 twice more. Break wire and fasten off.

FINISHING

Join the lobster clasp to one of the connector findings with the 5 mm jump ring. Thread one of the tail ends onto the sewing needle and sew the connector to the end of the choker. Join the other connector to the length of chain with the 7 mm jump ring and sew to the other end of the choker. Neaten ends and trim close to work.

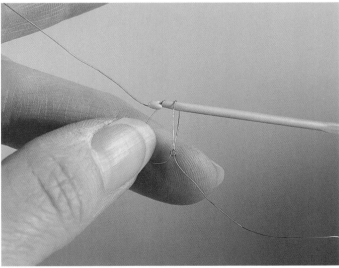

1 *Solomon knot stitch – Preparing to draw through the loop whilst keeping the single back loop separate from the front two threads.*

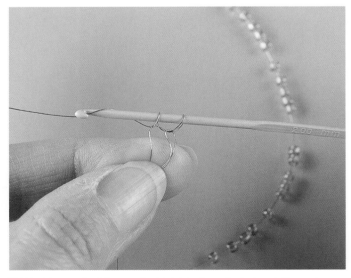

2 *Working a double crochet (dc) in the single back thread; preparing to draw through the last two loops on the hook.*

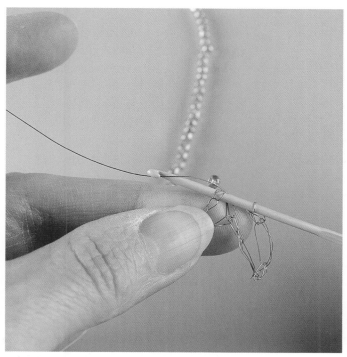

3 *Bdc – Inserting the hook in dc between third and fourth loops from the hook bringing in a bead and preparing to draw through the loop. Yoh and finish by drawing through the last 2 loops on the hook*

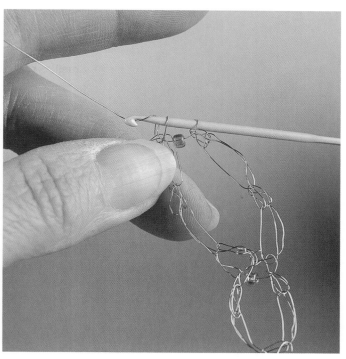

4 *After working 2 MSK's, miss two loops working a bead double crochet (Bdc) into the next double crochet (dc); preparing to draw through the last two loops on the hook.*

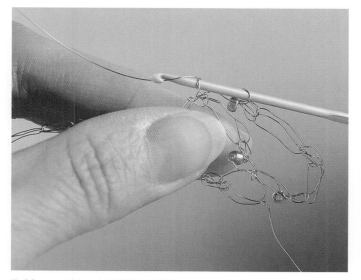

5 *After working 1 BESK, 1 ESK and 1 MSK, a bead double crochet (Bdc) is worked into dc between fourth and fifth loops; preparing to draw through the last two loops on the hook.*

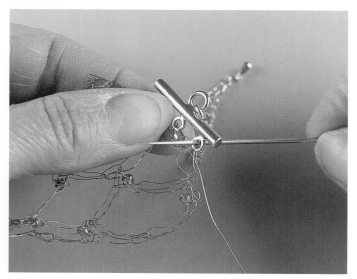

6 *Using the tail end to sew on a finding.*

Index

Acknowledgements

There are many people that I would like to thank for helping me to make this book possible. Firstly a big thanks to Diana Vernon, my colleague at South Thames College for recommending me to the publishers. Diana is a hugely talented bead-worker, who thankfully does not include crochet in her repertoire, otherwise this could have been her project!

The support of my students at South Thames College is invaluable; they keep me in touch with what can be achieved by beginners and they test my pattern writing skills to the limit. I owe a big thanks to Maurice who knows where to source everything and saved me a lot of legwork – you are a star!

Trish, Sarah, Fiona and Sue, my crochet and knitting group: we've been meeting for so many years – way before it was fashionable to 'knit & bitch'. Thanks for the honest feedback and for letting me bounce ideas off you all. Sorry I haven't been able to join the group every week whilst I've been hard at work on this project.

Finally, to my wonderful family: my children Bibi and Brutus have become expert at threading beads and picking up my spills, my partner Mark for keeping me fed and watered and for being a constant inspiration, and my mum and dad, who have always believed in me.